CATS 'n KITTENS

OVERLEAF: MAINE COON CAT

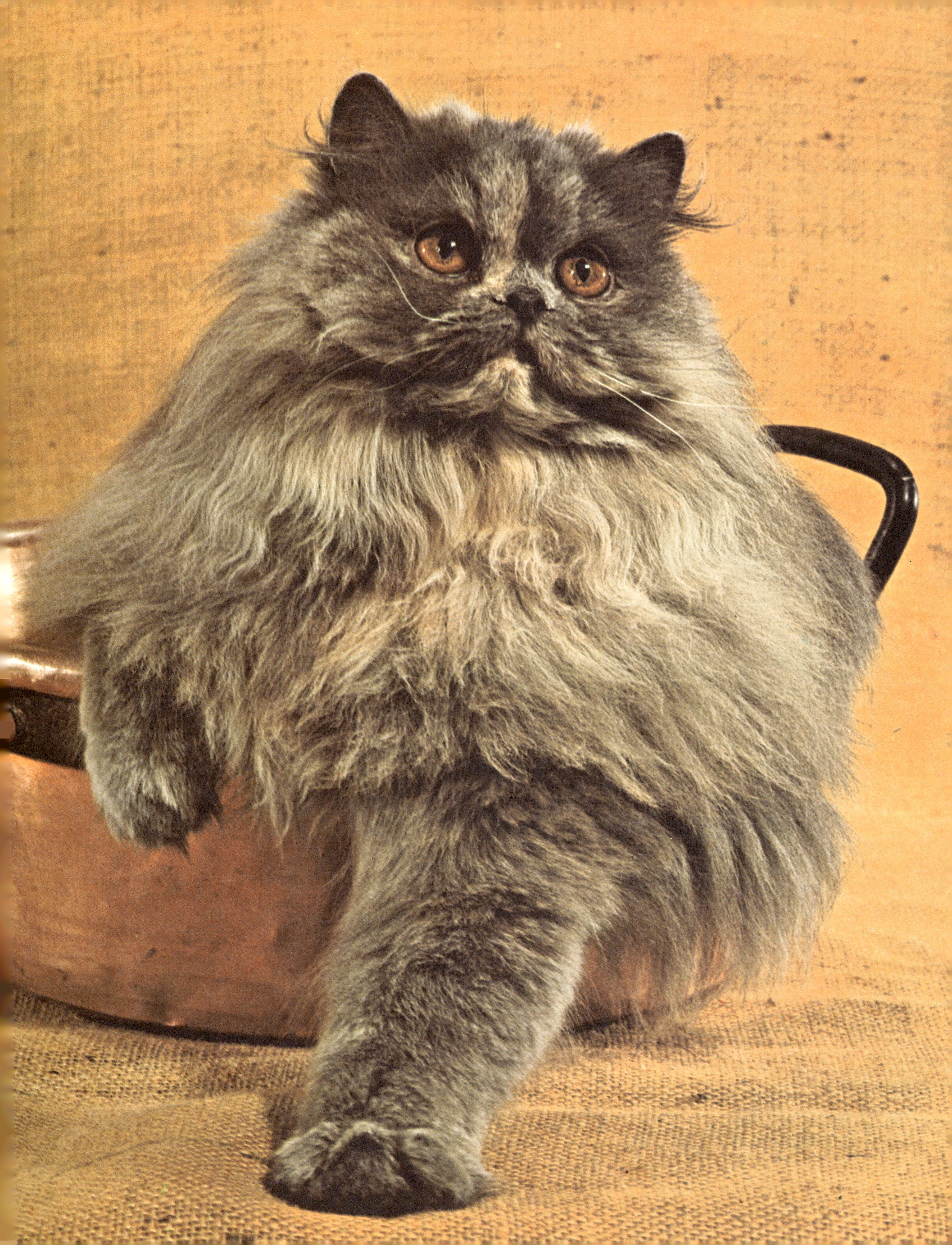

ABYSSINIAN KITTEN   WHITE PERSIAN KITTENS
RED PERSIAN KITTEN   SIAMESE SEAL-POINT KITTENS

OVERLEAF: PERSIAN BLUE CREAM

CATS 'n KITTENS

by Ted Allen

Photographs by Creszentia Anna Allen

ARCO PUBLISHING COMPANY, INC.
219 Park Avenue South, New York, N.Y. 10003

Published by Arco Publishing Company, Inc.
219 Park Avenue South, New York, N.Y. 10003

Copyright © 1972 by Arco Publishing Company, Inc.
All rights reserved

Library of Congress Catalog Card Number 73–186390
Regular Edition: ISBN 0-668-02599-9
Library Edition: ISBN 0-668-02730-4

Printed in the United States of America

ACKNOWLEDGMENTS

The authors would like to thank the owners, breeders, and trainers, and the following individuals and corporations who assisted and cooperated with them in producing this book:

American Cyanamid Company
Veterinary Professional Service Department
Princeton, New Jersey 08540
for permission to use portions of *Protect Your Pet*

Richard H. Gebhardt
The Cat Fanciers' Association, Inc.
Box P
Red Bank, New Jersey

Dr. E. Padwee, D.V.M.
245 Belleville Avenue
Belleville, New Jersey

Puss 'n Boots
Division of the Quaker Oats Company
Chicago, Illinois 60654
for permission to use portions of their cat booklet

Ralston Purina Company
Checkerboard Square
St. Louis, Missouri 63199
for permission to use portions of their cat booklet

Sharlene and William H. Starbuck
359 Overlook Drive
West Lafayette, Indiana
for permission to use portions of *Your New Kitten*

USV Pharmaceutical Corporation
Veterinary Products Division
800 Second Avenue
New York, N.Y. 10017
for permission to use portions of *A Cat Is to Love*

The Willamette Valley Cat Club
29960 Harvester Road
Malibu, California
for permission to use portions of *Manual of Cat Care*

BLUE PERSIAN

Contents

A Short History of the Cat	13
Choosing a Cat	29
The Cat's New Home	41
Good Grooming	47
Cats' Eyes	59
Choosing a Veterinarian	61
A Cat's Best Friend Is a Dog	65
The Outdoor Cat	67
Showing Your Cat	71
Classification of Cats	73
The Abyssinian Cat	75
The Burmese Cat	77
The Domestic Shorthair	79
The Himalayan Cat	81
The Korat Cat	83
The Manx Cat	85
The Persian Cat	87
The Rex Cat	89
The Russian Blue	91
The Siamese Cat	93
Glossary	94

HOUSEHOLD PET

CATS 'n KITTENS

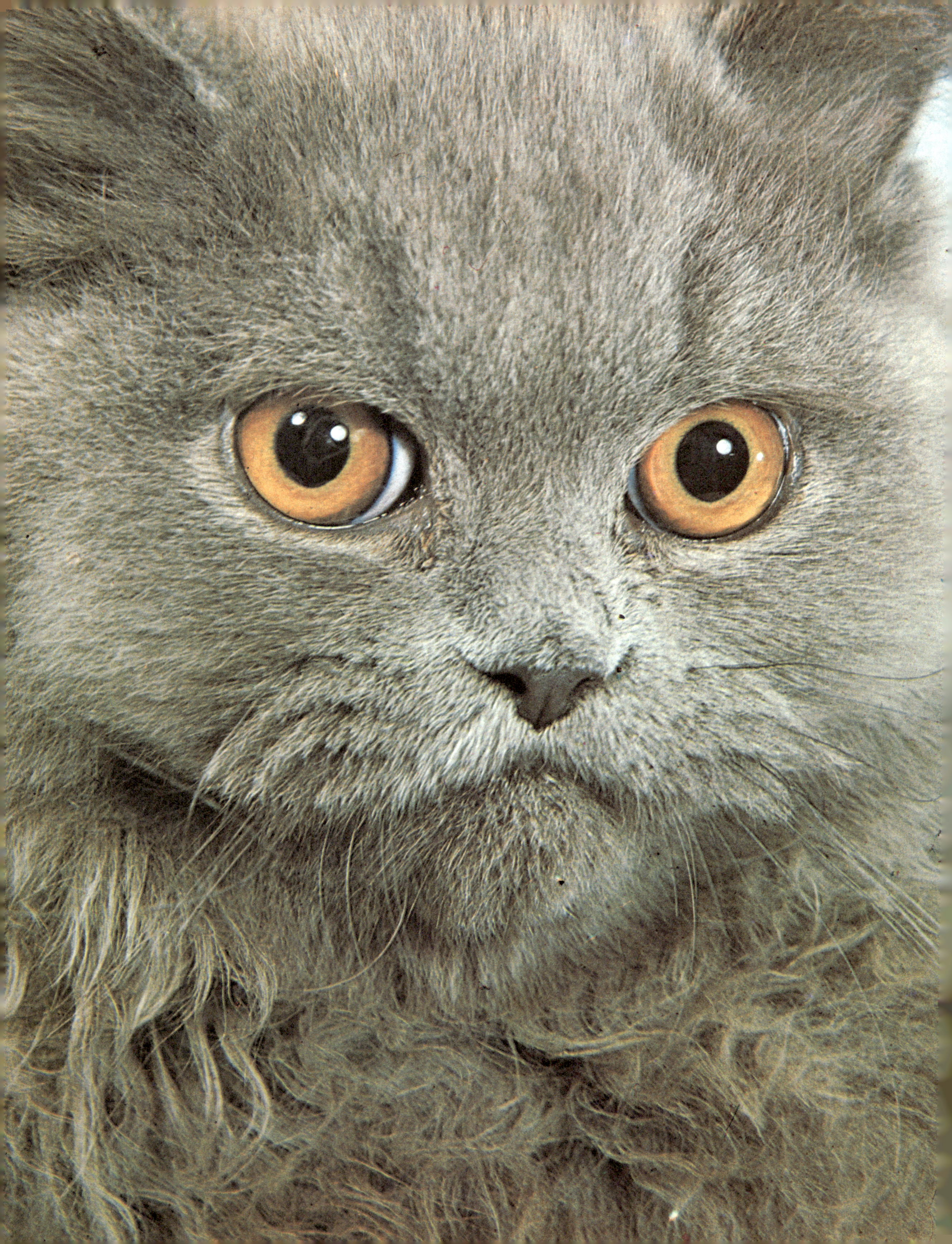

PERSIAN TABBY

A Short History of the Cat

No less an authority than Charles Darwin once stated that the origin of all domestic animals will probably remain forever vague.

If we are inclined to the fanciful, we can accept, perhaps, some of the legends which tell us of the cat's beginning. One of these concerns Noah, his Ark and the Great Flood. After weeks of floating on the flooded surface of the earth, the legend goes, the rats and mice began to multiply at such an alarming rate that the other animals were in danger. Noah saw that something must be done so he approached his lioness and passed his hand over her head three times. The lioness then sneezed mightily and there appeared in the aftermath the domestic cat, who from that day forward preyed on the rodents and kept their population in check.

Of course, such legends may capture the imagination but in our day of enlightenment we know that they are not true. To discover the origins of the domestic cat it is much wiser to turn to science and try to trace the history of the cat from the very beginning —some 40,000,000 years ago—shortly after mammals made their appearance on earth.

At that time, the earth was undergoing a change from the Eocene period to the Oligocene. The mammals—animals with hair and the characteristic of suckling their young—had recently evolved from lower forms. None of the new mammals was very large. Horses, for instance, were about the size of sheep and rhinoceroses were small, horse-like animals without horns.

Among the early mammals was one called *Miacis*. About the size of a polecat, *Miacis* lived in the trees. It had a long body but relatively short legs, such as some of the modern civets. This early mammal was the ancestor of all the later land-dwelling carnivores, or meat-eating mammals. These included the cats, as well as bears, raccoons, hyenas, dogs and others. In time, *Miacis* became more and more like modern civets. And then an astonishing thing happened. Suddenly—at least in terms of geological time—these primitive civets became cats. There is no clearcut line marking the change, but they did appear within a relatively brief span, unlike the development of other mammals which stretched over eons.

The two great cats of the time were called *Hoploohoneus* and *Dinictis*. Both made their appearance during the early Oligocene Age, and both were unmistakably cats. They had the feline shape, muscles, eyes and claws of cats and possessed long canine teeth. In time *Hoploohoneus* began to undergo a change. The canines grew longer and projected below the lower jaw in knife-like fashion.

Hoploohoneus developed very powerful muscles and kept growing in size until he became the largest and most fearsome cat ever to live—the saber-toothed tiger. His reign lasted until only about 20,000 years ago when he died out, chiefly because all the large sloths and other slow-moving animals he preyed upon became extinct first.

The other original cat—*Dinictis*—was also a large cat by today's standards, though not quite so im-

DOMESTIC SHORTHAIR HOUSEHOLD PET

MAINE COON CAT

mense as the saber-toothed. These true cats preyed on swift-moving animals such as three-toed horses and as a result were forced to rely on their wits as well as their muscles. Bones of both the true cats and the saber-tooth tigers have been found in the polar regions, Australia and North America, indicating that they lived together in the same areas.

Once the true cat was established on earth, it changed very little through the ages. There were developments, of course, the leopard acquired spots, the tiger stripes, and so on. But essentially their appearance and habits remain the same today as they were in prehistoric times. Even a domestic cat stalking a bird through the grass exhibits all the predatory characteristics of the *Dinictis*.

But when did cats first learn to live with man? The answer to that question is buried in history. It is known that the domestic cat has been around for thousands of years. It is thought that the Egyptians, who adored cats, first purchased the animal from Nubia some 5,000 years ago when it had already been well established in India and China. By 3,500 B.C. the cat was enjoying a luxurious life in Egypt. The early Egyptians often worshipped the cat as a god, probably because the animal had succeeded in ridding the people's granaries of rats and mice.

Cats were worshipped in Egypt until almost 400 A.D. Many steno carvings have been unearthed showing cats stretched out on rugs, eating fish and mice and, in general enjoying the leisurely life. Evidently, cats were everywhere in ancient Egypt—in the cities and the country, in poor homes and in palaces, where they were pampered with fish and bread soaked in milk.

When a cat died, the members of the family that owned him would shave their eyebrows and observe a lengthy, elaborate period of mourning. When a palace cat died, the entire populace would mourn. The cats were often mummified and buried beneath temples such as the one at Bubastis, which honored the cat goddess, Bast. Special cats were interred in the holy fields of Spees Artemides near the tombs of Beni Hasan.

Although cats were enormously popular with the Egyptians, few other peoples in the western world appreciated them. Perhaps one important reason for this is the natural dislike cats have for travel. Understandably, nomadic tribes would hardly provide the atmosphere for a pleasant relationship between man and cat.

The Golden Age of Greece knew no cats, as far as can be learned. When cats did arrive in Greece, the civilization had passed its peak and the animal was tolerated but hardly worshipped. The Greeks fashioned their gods after themselves, not after animals.

However, the Romans seemed to pick up where

RED PERSIAN TABBY

BLACK PERSIAN

the Egyptians had left off. The mighty Roman goddess of Liberty was depicted with a cup in one hand, a sceptre in the other and a cat at her feet. Indeed, historians tell us that several Roman legions marched off to conquer foreign territory with a cat blazoned on their shields and banners. One such legion, the *Alpini,* used as a symbol of its fighting prowess a battered old tomcat with one eye and one ear missing.

Meanwhile, back in Egypt, traders had found a ready market for cats in other lands that touched the Mediterranean. The export of cats became so great that the Egyptian rulers passed a law making it illegal to carry felines out of the country, but smugglers continued to do so and soon the rat-catching domestic cats became established in a number of European nations. They were not the first cats to appear in Europe, however. European wildcats—roughly the same size as the Egyptians domestics—already roamed the continent. With the establishment of the North African cat on the seacoast, it was inevitable that cross-breeding in the wild should occur. The result *Felis domestica* is the domestic cat of today.

The English word, "cat," comes from the Latin name *catus* given the animals by the Roman writer, Palladius, in the 4th Century. This name undoubtedly was an outgrowth of the Egyptian *kut,* which meant a male cat, and *kutta,* a female cat. Before that, the tame cat of Nubia was called *kadio*. And in Turkey, the animal was named *kedi.* The Greeks had a word for it too—*katta*. The sounds of today's words "cat" and "kitty" are not far removed from these ancient terms.

From the cat's heyday in ancient Egypt to its persecution in the Dark Ages, little is known of their existence. There are literally hundreds of years during which the comings and goings of cats was not recorded by historians. The animal's appearance was chronicled by a Welsh king, Howel the Good, who in the year 948 issued a law governing the market price of cats. This law makes it plain to us today that the Welsh kept cats as pets and valued them greatly, probably because the little animals were quite rare at the time. According to Howel's edict, the following prices were established:

1. A kitten was worth one penny when sold before its eyes were open.
2. The price would remain at twopence until it had caught its first mouse.
3. A grown cat was priced at fourpence.

In those days a penny was worth quite a lot of money. It could purchase, for instance, a lamb. For fourpence one could own a sheep or a goat, so you can see that the Welsh king placed a high value on the cats of the land.

Howel established certain standards for a cat to meet in order to command the full price. A cat had to be keen of eyesight and hearing. It also had to have all its claws and be capable of raising kittens. If the

BLUE PERSIAN

animal did not meet all these requirements, the law demanded that one-third of the sale price be refunded. Howel's code also had a section dealing with cat owners and cat thieves. As to the former, it required that "the seller is to answer for her not going caterwauling every moon." And serious penalties were imposed upon anyone caught stealing a cat from the royal granaries. The criminal was required to pay a pile of grain equal in height to the length of the cat, including its tail, while the cat was suspended from its tail.

The Welsh code also included the presence of a cat, along with nine buildings, one plow, one kiln (an oven), one churn, one bull, one cock, and one herdsman, as necessary to establish the legal status of a hamlet. Divorce was uncommon in those days, but in case of marital separation it was stipulated that the husband was to receive the cat, even though all other household items were divided equally.

The early Moslems, too, treated cats with care. One story tells of the time Muezza, the pet cat of Mohammed, was curled up asleep on the sleeves of its master's robe. Suddenly, Mohammed, who had been watching his pet fondly, was called to a council meeting. Rather than disturb Muezza's nap he cut off his sleeve.

A 12th-century Moslem leader named el-Daher-Beybars was particularly enamoured of cats. He ordered in his will that a lush garden, called *Gheyt-el-Quottah,* or cat's orchard, to be built. The garden, situated near Cairo, was for the enjoyment of all the homeless cats in the area. Food was placed in the outer court of the garden and before long stray cats from miles around began to frequent the place. This oasis for cats was maintained in Egypt until 1870 when funds for the food and upkeep ran out.

The poor cat suffered mightily during the Dark Ages of Europe. Cats became the symbol of evil and were tortured and killed indiscriminately. They were, for example, thought to be the handmaidens of witches and the animal form most likely to be occupied by the devil on his visits to this world.

In France, particularly, cats were horribly mistreated. Frenchmen considered it morally just to toss cats by the basketload into roaring flames. The festival of St. John was especially marked by its sacrifice of cats. The practice continued until 1604 when King Henry IV was persuaded by a young lad to issue a royal decree forbidding the ceremony. The youngster who saved the cats was later to attain the throne himself as Louis XIII. Cats in Picardy were rounded up for weeks ahead of time and held captive until the first Sunday of Lent. They were thrown into a roaring fire on that holy day after a parade through the village by the townspeople. Local musicians entertained the populace as the screaming cats were tossed into the fires.

Flemish peasants carried the town's cats to the top of the highest steeple and dropped them to the pavement below. A statute was finally passed in 1618 prohibiting the people from heaving the cats off the tower in the village of Ypres on the second Wednesday in Lent, a practice they had been observing for years.

In England, cats were used for target practice by that country's archers. The cats were shoved into leathern bottles and set up on a fence to await the sting of the arrows.

That cats should have been mistreated so during the Dark Ages is understandable when we realize that man has been both attracted and repelled by these animals through the ages. Mythology and primitive psychology have both contributed to the mystic symbolism that has grown up around cats. Even today we have superstitions concerning cats. Many people, for instance, believe that if a black cat crosses their path they will suffer poor fortune. And our traditional Halloween stories cite cats as the companions of witches and spirits.

One of the most unfortunate connections (for the cat) in the eyes of man is that of the cat and the moon. In primitive times, the moon was once a respectable and powerful god-force. But after Christianity's roots had become well established, the force of the moon as a deity was greatly diminished. In effect, all that was left to represent the former power of the moon in pagan thought were witches.

HOUSEHOLD PET

SIAMESE

The association of the moon with cats probably begins with the cat's eyes. Their strange, beautiful luminosity and mystic ability to penetrate the darkest nights thrust fear into the hearts of men who lived by the sun. Primitive men believed, then, that the cat had some natural link with whatever mysterious powers dwelt in the night. Then, too, the natural position of a female cat while suckling her kittens suggests the moon's crescent.

The silent walk of a cat, the ability to leap suddenly to a high place as though the animal were being guided by some unseen force brought awe to the eyes of early man. Our ancestors also may have had the feeling that a cat sees, hears and knows things that humans do not. For instance, the stare of a cat is intense but it is sometimes difficult to determine just what the cat is looking at. It was easy, then, for early man—filled with superstition—to conclude that the cat was seeing something which man could not see. When a cat in intense concentration sprang at nothing, as cats sometimes do, it was thought they were striking at ghosts.

As mentioned, in the Dark Ages cats had become the symbol of evil and were killed and tortured. This practice continued throughout Europe, especially with the widespread recognition of witchcraft on the part of the church. Sometimes the cat itself was thought to be the witch; at other times, the animal was merely the evil companion of the human accused of being a witch. In the 200 years covering the 16th and 17th Century it is believed that some 200,000 witches were executed in Great Britain and Europe. In many of those cases, cat-companions were also killed.

The witches, when brought to justice, frequently incriminated their cats, and records of the time are filled with this "proof" of the evil life of a cat. For example, a famous witch in Scotland, Isabel Gowdie, confessed that many of her companion witches prowled in the form of cats, even though she herself preferred to take the shape of a hare. Isabel was burned at the stake in 1662.

In 1566, it is recorded, a group of cats engaged in nocturnal and mystic rites in a forest in France was surprised by a posse of farmers. The cats turned on the farmers, clawing and biting them, but the men managed to escape. The next morning a dozen women in the village were found to have bruises and scratches on their bodies. They confessed that they had, indeed, met as cats in the dark of night the evening before.

Uncounted stories and legends about cats were told during the Dark Ages in all the nations of Europe. Perhaps the most famous is the tale of "The King of the Cats." A traveler on a highway stumbles upon a procession of cats at midnight. The cats are carrying a tiny coffin with a crown set atop it. The terrified traveler rushes into the next village and tells his tale to the master of the first cottage he sees. When he finishes the story, the villager's cat, which has been

HOUSEHOLD PET

BLACK PERSIAN

HOUSEHOLD PET

TORTOISESHELL PERSIAN

napping near the fire, suddenly springs up with a screech and shouts: "Then I am the King of the Cats." Whereupon, to the utter amazement of the traveler and the villager alike, the cat scrambles up the chimney and out of the house in a rush to claim its crown.

There is also the story of the young man whose beautiful bride reveals, on her wedding night, her true nature. She leaps from his arms to chase a mouse that has scampered across the floor.

In many of those stories, the cat—believed, of course, to be a witch—is given the power of speech. This ability always reveals his true identity as a witch. In one, a woman who is cooking an omelet is startled by a strange cat that enters her kitchen and remarks, "It is done, turn it over." She hurls the omelet in the face of the cat, sending it scampering away. The next day, she notices a bad burn on the face of her neighbor.

With the coming of the Renaissance, cats fared better. The French—in particular, perhaps because they had treated the felines so miserably, took pains to make the cat feel welcome. In many rural areas, French peasants constructed small hinged openings in the doors of their homes to allow the family cat to enter and leave at will. But these *chatieres,* as they were called, vanished almost as fast as they had appeared. The reason? The cat had trained the peasants to let him in and out at his whim.

Suddenly, everyone in France loved cats. Rich and poor, nobles and commoners alike harbored the pets. They were particularly at home in the court of Louis XIV amid the gilt and splendor of the palace of Versailles.

Young Louis XV was in council with his ministers one day when a kitten invaded the chambers, leaped on the table and scattered state documents in every direction. The king, only eight years old at the time, doubled up in laughter while his cabinet members scurried to and fro to retrieve the documents and corner the frightened kitten. It was later suggested to the king that the kitten be adopted as a permanent member of the council since it had undoubtedly proven itself more competent in state matters than several of the ministers.

The church, which had been largely responsible for the dilemma of cats during the earlier witch hunts, also began to view cats with more tender attitudes. Cardinal Richelieu was especially fond of kittens. He kept several constantly at his side, replacing them when they grew to three months of age. Cardinal Mazarin, on the other hand, was fond of cats of all ages and always had several in his household. And Abbe Galiani was once so angered over the disappearance of one of his favorite cats that he fired his entire staff. Across the channel, the Church of England has had more than its share of cat-lovers among its clergy. Among the better known was Bishop Thirlwall who had several cats and permitted them to make them-

KORAT

selves comfortable on the arms of his chair while he was at dinner. Once, when a visitor suggested that the Bishop would be more comfortable in a nearby easy chair, the cleric replied, "Don't you see who already occupies it?" He pointed to one of his pets comfortably curled up in the middle of the cushion.

Since the Age of Enlightenment, cats have enjoyed a high position of acceptance in most of the civilized world.

From the foregoing history of cats in general it can be seen that much of the lineage of the animals is shrouded in mystery. Such is the case also when one attempts to trace the history of a single breed of cats. Let us examine closely the lineage of the Abyssinian, the so-called "sacred cat of Egypt," and we will discover that its history is incomplete at best.

The slender, sleek Aby is regarded by zoologists, geneticists and many breeders as the eldest breed of domestic cat. But is it actually a descendant of the "sacred cat of Egypt?" It is very similar in appearance to the images of the sacred cat that archeologists have unearthed from Egyptian tombs and ruins. These paintings, statues and plaques depicting the sacred cat show an animal with a lithe, long body, a whiplike tail, large eyes and alert ears. These characteristics are very much a part of today's Aby.

However, pinpointing its origins to the region once known as Abyssinia is foolhardy, at best. Abyssinia today is known as Ethiopia, a nation whose citizens do not keep many domestic cats as pets. The Aby does resemble some small wild cats in North Africa, and it may be that the Aby developed from those wild creatures—long after the "sacred cat of Egypt" was revered in ancient Cairo.

At any rate, the first positive fact in the lineage of the Abyssinian occurred in 1868. This date marked the arrival of the Aby in the western world. According to early accounts, Mrs. Barrett-Lennard first imported an Abyssinian cat to England in that year. It is doubtful that the lady actually traveled to Africa to obtain her precious cat, since that part of the world was extremely hostile to white men, let alone a white woman.

In order to establish the bridge between Africa

MAINE COON CAT

HOUSEHOLD PET KITTENS

and England across which the Abyssinian cat made its way to our culture, it is worthwhile to recount briefly some of the history of the time. Abyssinia, prior to the latter half of the 18th Century, was a badly divided nation. The real power lay in the hands of the rulers of two kingdoms, Tigre and Amhara, and they were constantly fighting each other for supremacy of the land. A man named Lij Kasa, who later became Emperor Theodore II and reigned from 1855 to 1868, was named chief of the kingdom of Kwara after the death of his uncle. Viewing the turmoil in his native land with alarm, he set out to unify the country. His first conquest was that of Amhara, one of the two most powerful kingdoms. He subsequently beat the armies of Tigre on the field of battle and in 1855 subdued the last independent kingdom, Shea.

With his nation unified under single rule, Theodore set out to modernize the country. He welcomed European artisans and engineers to aid him in his task. Theodore did a remarkable job, with the help of the Europeans, and perhaps this success gave him some delusions of grandeur. At any rate he dispatched a message to Queen Victoria in England in 1867 requesting she send him a shipload of agricultural tools. This request was logical enough, but some historians tell us that in the same letter Theodore asked the Queen for her hand in marriage.

A reply from the queen, astounded by the impudence of this "savage," was not forthcoming, and Theodore felt slighted. Whereupon he ordered the arrest of some 60 British, French and German subjects working in his land, including the British consul, Capt. Charles Duncan Cameron. He refused steadfastly all demands that he release his prisoners.

In July of 1867, Sir Robert Napier led an invasion force of about 32,000 British troops overland to the camp of Theodore. The route included a march of some 400 miles across mountainous and uncharted wilderness inhabited by savage tribes. But the British pressed on, gaining safe passage through the tribal territories by giving trinkets to the chiefs. As they approached Theodore's camp, word of their arrival set the Ethiopian ruler into a frenzy. He committed suicide by shooting himself with a revolver which had been a gift to him from Queen Victoria.

The significance of this event in history, from the point of view of the Aby, is this: It is most likely that many of the British soldiers took into their care the young cats or kittens that seemed so friendly and were so easy to domesticate. The British army left Ethiopia in May of 1868 doubtless accompanied back

BLUE PERSIAN

SIAMESE BLUE-POINT

PERSIAN SMOKE

to the British Isles by an unknown number of Abyssinian cats.

As noted before, the earliest record of an Aby in Britain was that belonging to Mrs. Barrett-Lennard. The year was 1868, the same year that Sir Robert's victorious army returned to the homeland.

Unaccountably, however, there is little mention of the Aby for another 30 years. They are listed for the first time as a separate breed in 1882 but it is not until 1900 that cat-fanciers pay any attention at all to the breed. At the turn of the century, the term "Abyssinian" was dropped, replaced by the term "ticked." The cats themselves became known as "British Ticks" or "Bunny Cats," the latter in reference to the Aby's fur which resembles that of a wild rabbit.

These cats were ticked. That is, the tip of the hair was flecked with blackish or dark brown coloring. Some of the best Abys today have about three bands of brown or orange shades, with the darkest lying at the tip of the hair. Frequently, however, these early "British Ticks" were more mottled than ticked. Sometimes today a cold-tone gray creeps into the Abyssinian strain, the result of unfortunate breeding during the early period.

PERSIAN MOTHER WITH KITTENS

SHADED SILVER PERSIAN

SHADED SILVER PERSIAN MALE

PERSIAN KITTEN

The popularity of the Abyssinian in England was a long time coming. By 1937, there were only 92 of the breed registered. Strangely enough, however, just as one war was responsible for the introduction of the Aby to the west, another war seemed responsible for increasing its popularity. When the Italians invaded Ethiopia in 1935, British cat-fanciers sympathetic to the cause of Emperor Haile Selassie began to value the Abyssinian cat more highly.

Records show that the first known Abyssinian cats to appear in the United States was a pair exhibited in Boston in 1909 by a Miss Jane Cathcart of Oradell, N.J. Where they came from is uncertain.

On July 7, 1935, a female Abyssinian, Addis Ababa, was born in the U.S.—the first native Aby. The kitten died several weeks later, however. Two years later, the prime Abyssinian of Great Britain, named Champion Ras Seyum, was especially imported to be mated with an American Aby, Weedrooffe Ena. The move was reported in all the cat publications of the time and a color photograph of Ras Seyum appeared in the National Geographic magazine of November, 1938. The publicity served to boost the Abyssinian into the mainstream of American life. More and more Abys were imported from England and they began to appear all over the U.S. Today there are Abyssinian breeders in all 50 states and each season finds more exhibitions of Abys than the previous.

RED PERSIAN KITTEN

HOUSEHOLD PET

HOUSEHOLD PETS

WHITE PERSIAN WITH BLUE EYES

MAINE COON CAT

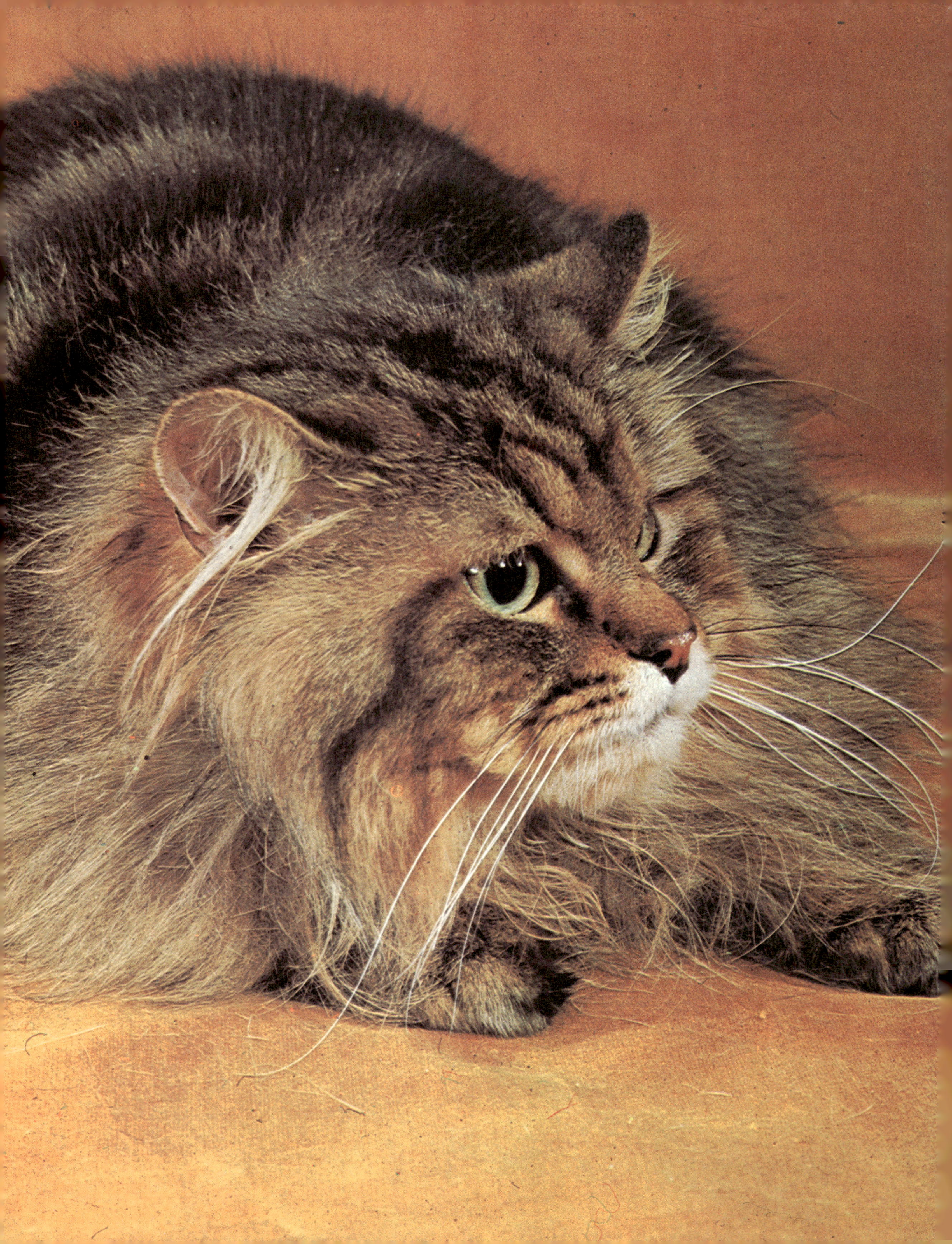

BROWN PERSIAN TABBY

Choosing a Cat

There are many kinds of cats—expensive ones and inexpensive ones, purebreds and so-called domestic cats whose ancestry has been completely lost. Choosing the one cat that best suits your needs is not a simple task, for mismatched cats and people are miserable together. But the right cat will fit well into your pattern of living and will offer hours of amusement and companionship.

Cat Owner

It has been said that there are three kinds of cat owners. One is the type of person who will do anything for his pet. This is a cowardly approach. This person will turn his entire house and living habits upside down to please his cat, allowing the little animal to mooch his food, claw his furniture and shred his rugs. Usually, the owner winds up with frayed nerves and a demolished house, while the cat, lacking guidance, becomes the moodiest of creatures. Any kind of cat, even the most docile Siamese, will turn into the monster described under such conditions.

The second type of cat owner does only the things absolutely necessary to keep his pet alive and to maintain order in the household. He lays out a tray of food for his cat once a day and puts him out at night, but that is about all he does. Under such a live-and-let live arrangement, neither cat nor owner gets much from the relationship. Any reasonably healthy cat will suit this owner, for the cat's personality and that of its so-called master will never intertwine.

The third type of owner, however, places a high value on his cat and the relationship he enjoys with his pet. He will not permit the cat to dictate the terms of the relationship, but neither will he allow the cat to be almost totally ignored. He takes good care of his pet's physical needs and develops the cat's personality by disciplining him. Here is an owner who respects his cat, and the cat, in turn, will respect him.

Obviously, the last type of owner is the best type. The first type is not really the owner; the cat seems to own him. The second fellow is so aloof that it is a wonder that he chose to have a cat in the first place; he could do just as well with a pet cockroach.

The Best Cats

A cat is a particularly strong-willed creature and it is pointless to try to radically change its character. Thus, the wise cat owner will know in advance just what kind of cat the cute little kitten he has acquired will grow up to be. There is only one proven way to determine this: by selecting a pedigreed breed whose behavior can be predicted. The advantage of buying a pedigree is simple: his heritage is a guarantee of his personality. The pedigreed cat will develop along predictable lines and will not undergo any major change in personality as he grows older.

Other Cats

On the other hand, the development of the alley cat is unpredictable. There is no guarantee that the kitten's personality will remain the same throughout life; in fact, the odds are that it will not. It is extremely difficult for the prospective cat owner to inspect a cattery-full of cuddly kittens and turn any one of them down. At that age, all cats are equally adorable. But, when armed with the knowledge that they will mature differently, the wisest course is to select a purebred. Otherwise, you may end up with a difficult strong-minded cat that does not suit your personality at all.

Of course, if a domestic cat is selected, chance plays a big factor in its development. Some domestic cats will mature well and make ideal pets. But, there is no way of insuring this as there is with pedigrees. Then, too, your cat may not be obtained through a pet shop but from a private individual whose cat has recently had a litter. Unless the cat's lineage is known, the same element of chance holds forth. And if you happen to take in a stray there is absolutely no surefire way to predict its development.

Pedigreed cats are divided into two major classifications; longhair and shorthair. There are few longhair breeds, the Persian being the most popular, and several shorthairs. The traits of each are listed elsewhere in this book.

PERSIAN BLUE WITH COPPER EYES

WHITE PERSIAN

Where to Obtain Cats

Cats may be obtained from a variety of sources, ranging from the highly professional show breeder, amateur breeders, pet shops, private individuals who find themselves with a surplus of kittens, and local animal pounds. The quality of your pet will depend to a great extent on the source. Only the professional show breeders and a few pet shops that sell show stock maintain rigid standards of quality.

It is important to keep in mind that simply labeling a cat a Siamese, for example, is not enough. There are good purebreds and there are bad purebreds. Since a professional breeder depends upon his sales to enhance his reputation, they are generally a reliable source.

You can judge for yourself the quality of a particular breeder's litters by viewing them at local cat shows. But, although you can make a selection at the show (you may be persuaded to, in fact) it is wisest to merely take note of the offerings and visit the breeder who interests you after the show has closed. In this way, you will have more time to select your cat and more time to do some comparison shopping.

Pet shows are listed in most cat-fancying magazines. Breeders also advertise in these magazines and you might try writing some of them to get information on their stock and prices.

Cats purchased from a professional show breeder may cost $75 or $100 or more, but the cost brings with it a guarantee of health and predictable development. Professional breeders rarely advertise in news-

BLUE PERSIAN KITTEN

papers. The ads you see in your local paper are often those of second-rate breeders and private individuals. Although the price quoted in these ads may be lower than those of the show breeders, so too is the quality of the kittens they have to offer. If the initial cost of buying a kitten is too much, you will probably be better off with a stray or domestic cat as a pet. Some of these animals make better pets than a poorly bred Siamese.

SELECTING A PET SHOP

If you decide to purchase your cat at a pet shop, there are certain things you should look for. First of all, there are very few establishments that deal exclusively in cats. Most pet shops sell dogs, cats, tropical fish, parakeets, turtles and other pets. Yours is a better pet shop if it at least has a separate section set aside for the care and grooming of cats. Such isolation will protect them from the barking of the dogs, which may upset them.

Your pet shop should also have a clean appearance, both to the sense of sight and to smell. Good sanitary practices by a pet shop owner will protect the health of the cats, as well as be more pleasing to the customer. Make sure the cages, at least, are kept clean. If there is spilled food and water, matted hair and other debris, quickly turn your back and exit the store. If the cages appear clean, however, next check the litter trays, which should contain commercial litter, not shredded newspaper. There should be no heavy accumulation of waste material. Also take notice of the type of food being fed the cats and whether there is ample clean water in the cages.

The area should also be well ventilated or air conditioned. Many germs are airborne and can be transmitted from one animal to another even though there is no direct contact. Ventilation helps prevent this.

The store owner or his clerks should not handle more than one animal at a time. This is very important in keeping all the animals healthy. The person who handles three or four cats may be responsible for spreading some disease from an ill cat to a healthy one. This rule also applies to the customer. If the shop owner permits you to handle his pets one after another, be suspect. You can spread these diseases as much as anyone.

EXAMINING A CAT

If you are particularly interested in one of the cats you see at a pet store or at a professional breeder's, you must examine the animal carefully before you decide to purchase it.

First, pick up the kitten or cat and feel along the spine and shoulder blades. If there is little flesh, the cat may be suffering from malnutrition, worms or some other disease. Feel all four of the legs and be

PERSIAN BLUE KITTEN

HOUSEHOLD PETS

SHADED SILVER PERSIAN KITTENS

TIGER YELLOW KITTENS

TIGER YELLOW KITTENS WITH MOTHER

HOUSEHOLD PETS

ABYSSINIAN KITTENS

certain that they are muscular and firm. Bow legs are usually a sign of rickets. The cat's stomach should be firm and smooth. If it is bloated or shrunken, there is something wrong. Hold the cat high and examine the anus. This should be clean, with no signs of diarrhea or tenderness.

A cat's eyes tell much about his general condition. They should be straight and bright. If there is redness in the corners or around the lids, it is usually an indication of conjunctivitis or a vitamin deficiency. Running eyes indicate a respiratory infection, worms or fungus.

The nose should be dry. If the cat is sniffling, this is a sure sign of one disease or another. If there are scabs or scaly markings on the nose it may mean that the cat has recently had a fungus infection.

The mouth of your cat should be firm, neither drooping nor sagging along the lips. With your fingers, press open the mouth and examine the teeth and gums. Sore, red or bruised gums are a positive indication of illness, as are missing teeth—unless it is a teething kitten.

The cat's ears should be clean and the tips of them should be free of any dry patches of skin or scales.

The neck should be firm with solid flesh extending up from the shoulder blades. Feel carefully in this area for any scaly patches of skin which could result from fungus or a vitamin deficiency.

The paws should be neat and the pads soft. Examine each paw carefully to determine whether any of the claws are broken.

In addition to this detailed inspection, take a general overall look at the cat you have selected. It should have the appearance of being healthy and well kept. The coat should be smooth and silky, with a soft texture. The coat of a shorthair cat lies smoothly against the body, while the coat of a Persian stands up in soft fluffs. The animal should be alert, not listless and the posture should be erect, with a straight back and a full tail.

RED PERSIAN TABBY

JUDGING A CAT'S PERSONALITY

Determining the personality of a cat is difficult in a single meeting, yet there are some objective signs to look for. Again, the most important factor is the cat's lineage. If this is known, then it is certain the kitten will develop into the same sort of cat his parents are. Here are some other traits to look for:

The cat should be lively and friendly. If it is a kitten, there should be absolutely no signs of fear. In any case, it should be receptive to petting and gentle han-

PERSIAN KITTENS WITH MOTHER

HOUSEHOLD PETS, TIGER GREY AND WHITE

dling. If it spits or squirms, it may be difficult for you to break through such a nasty disposition.

If the cat you are interested in is a pedigree, be sure it shows the qualities of its particular breed. Bad specimens of pedigreed cats do occur, mainly as the result of improper or careless breeding. Once you become familiar with a particular breed, you will be able to detect kittens that have been poorly bred.

A cat's sex contributes virtually nothing to its personality. This is to say male and female cats exhibit the same affection and playfulness.

GUARANTEES

Once you have selected, examined and decided on a particular cat, there are certain guarantees which you should insist upon. Quality pet shops and professional breeders will usually give a minimum guarantee of one month from purchase date. This guarantee should be in writing, signed by the owner and should specifically protect you against the loss of the kitten due to a disease or hereditary defect. Some shops offer guarantees for a longer period of time—as much as eight months, which is when a kitten attains maturity. Guarantees are especially important in covering the first month, however. You have no way of determining whether the kitten you have just bought is incubating some disease, despite the cleanliness of the shop. Feline diseases incubate for at least six days, and if your kitten comes down with a cold and complications you will spend a fortune at the vet's unless you have a guarantee.

MEDICAL HISTORY

When purchasing your cat you should find out if the animal has had its full series of permanent feline enteritis shots. This is a fatal disease in cats but the vaccine has proved its worth in a quarter century of use. (Enteritis responds to antibiotics, it was found recently, so many catteries do not inoculate kittens.) If temporary serum inoculations have been given your cat, you will have to take the animal to the vet for the permanent type. It is far wiser to insist this be done before you make your purchase.

You should also learn the age and sex of your kitten when buying him. To those unfamiliar with cats, determining their sex is not an easy task, especially in the case of kittens. Your cat's birthdate should be noted so that you will know when it is time to have him altered and when he can start eating on an adult schedule.

Ideally, you should not purchase a kitten younger than two months old. Up to this time it should remain with its mother. On the other hand, buying a cat that is older than one year may be inviting trouble. A mature cat may bring with it problems that its previous owners could not cope with—hence the reason he has been placed in the marketplace.

WHITE PERSIAN KITTEN

HOUSEHOLD PETS, TIGER GREY AND WHITE

HOUSEHOLD PET,
BROWN TABBY

PERSIAN CREAM

ABYSSINIAN KITTENS

Pedigreed History

Here are six simple, objective questions to apply to pedigree papers to make certain they are authentic and valuable:

1. Are the papers on an official form of one of the cat-fancying associations and do they bear the group's letterhead or seal?
2. Is the ancestry traced back at least five generations?
3. Is the name of each ancestor preceded by the name of the cattery to which it belonged?
4. Is the cat's registration number included with the name?
5. Are champions, double champions and triple champions included on the pedigree? (These are abbreviated Ch., Dbl. Ch. and Tr. Ch. before the name of the cat.)
6. Is the pedigree signed by the breeder?

Cats from Other Sources

So far, we have talked principally of the pedigreed cats you may purchase from a pet store or a show breeder. But what of the strays, the alley cats, the cute little kittens advertised in the local newspaper?

First, it is important to remember that there is no guarantee that the cuddly, playful kitten will grow up into the sort of cat you want. He may or he may not—it's always a risk. But if you cannot afford a pedigreed cat, you may wish to adopt a cat from the local pound, humane society or similar agency.

Many of the rules we outlined in purchasing a pedigreed cat apply. For example, the kennels or pound you visit should be clean and antiseptic and well ventilated. The cats should be separated from the other animals. The litter trays should be filled with commercial litter; there should be enough food and water to insure the health of the cats. If the place you are adopting a cat does not even approach such standards of quality and cleanliness, forget the whole idea or try another agency.

Of course, you should examine the cat you select just as carefully as you would a pedigree to get a line on the general health and well being of the animal.

Sometimes you may discover a stray cat lingering outside your kitchen door. He is there, not because he is particularly attracted to the hominess of your yard but because he is sensitive to the odors of cooking drifting out of your kitchen.

If the cat appears well groomed and healthy, chances are that he has wandered off from some home in the neighborhood. You should make an effort to discover where his owners live, either through inquiries made of the neighbors or through an advertisement placed in the lost and found columns of your local newspaper. If you are unable to locate the cat's rightful owners, you may either take him to the pound or permanently adopt him.

Even if the owners cannot be located right away, however, you should contact the pound and the police and give them a full description of the wanderer. If the previous owner is at all interested, chances are that he has already reported the missing cat to the police.

Let us assume, however, that you have made every effort to locate the owner and have been unsuccessful, and so you decide to adopt the stray. Take him to the veterinarian at once for a thorough going over. Since you have no way of determining whether the cat has received its permanent feline enteritis vaccine, it should be given at this time. And remember, although quality pedigreed cats are undoubtedly the best kind to have, a good alley cat can be much more rewarding as a pet than a poorly pedigreed animal.

BURMESE KITTENS

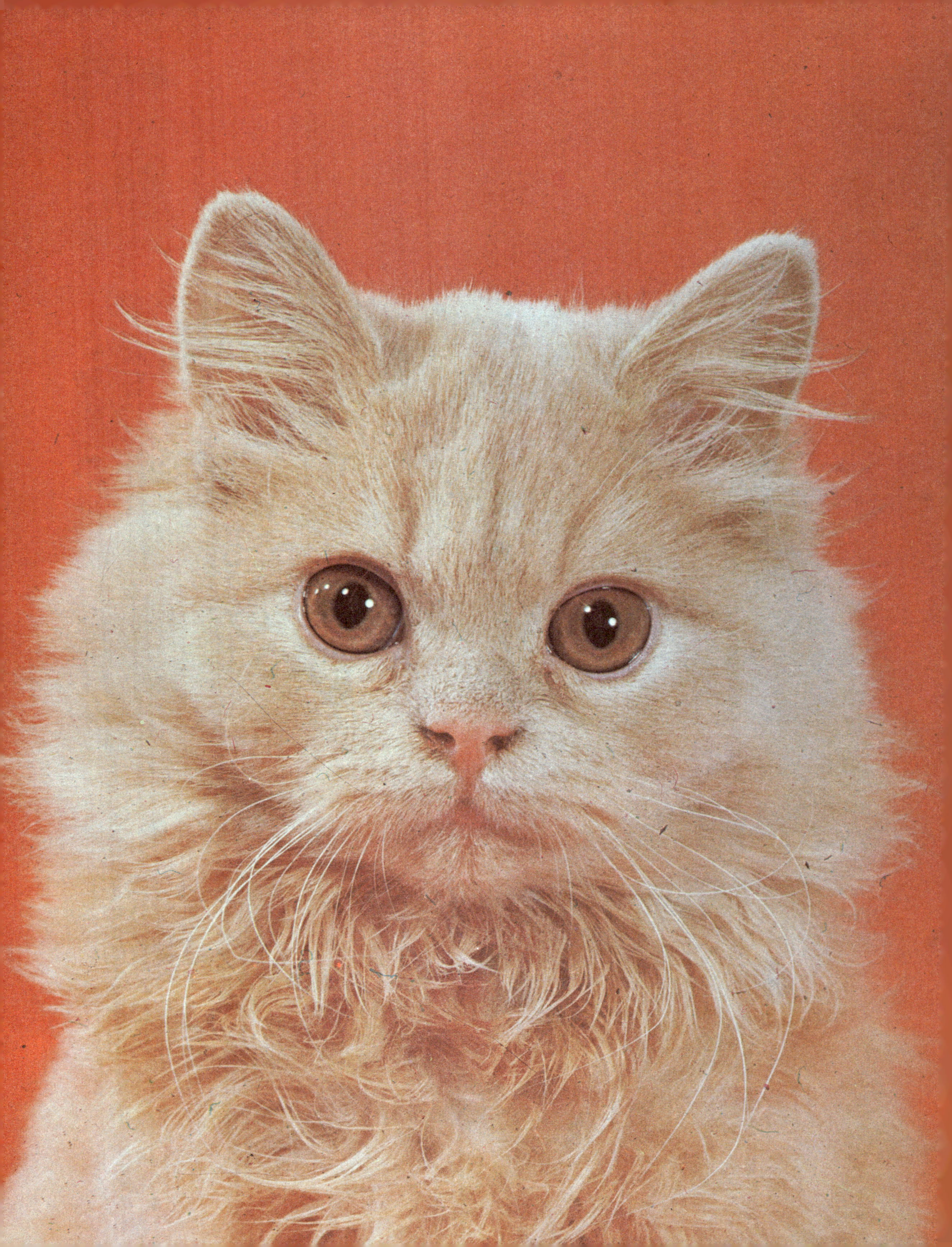

PERSIAN TABBY KITTEN

The Cat's New Home

Now that you have studied cats and selected the one you want (or have taken in a stray), you are going to find that certain duties will be required of you as a brand new cat owner. The first 24 hours of a cat's life in a new home can be trying on both cat and owner. If your new pet is merely a kitten, he is likely to be completely bewildered, having been snatched from the security of his cage and possibly his mother.

It is best not to expect too much from your kitten upon arrival in the household. He is naturally curious and will want to explore everything. Don't let him. Confine him to just one room, at least for the first day and night that he is in the house. This will help your kitten adjust to his new surroundings. If he is permitted to wander helter-skelter throughout your house or apartment, it will take him much longer to adjust. Confining him to just one room will also help prevent accidents when your kitten must answer the call of nature. Cats are much easier to housebreak than dogs and are naturally disposed toward cleanliness.

There should be two items set up in advance: a litter tray and a water dish. When you first bring your cat home, place him in the litter tray at once. If your kitten has been purchased from a good breeder or cattery he probably already knows the purpose of a litter tray. By placing him in it immediately you are serving notice on him that this is where it is located and this is where he is expected to perform.

Litter Boxes

The best litter trays, or boxes, are made of heavy plastic and are about five inches high, 15 inches wide and 18 inches long. Plastic trays may be easily cleaned in scalding hot water and they will not rust or absorb odors. Probably the best place to put the litter box is in the bathroom, but wherever you decide to put it be sure to keep it in that one spot so as not to confuse your cat.

The litter box should be lined with some sort of absorbent material. Sawdust, sand and shredded newspapers may be used, but each has its drawbacks. Sawdust is liable to be tracked all over the living room carpet. Sand also is easily tracked and does a poor job of absorbing odors so that the litter box must be cleaned often. Shredded newspapers are certainly the most easily available of materials, but they absorb odors poorly and must be changed daily.

There is available on the market commercial cat litter, which is a clay product and is highly absorbent. A good commercial litter should last five days, when used by only one cat.

Cats willingly use a litter tray and, with the exception of Persians, rarely forget their training. If they do forget, it is usually an indication of either illness or confusion over the location of the litter tray. Sometimes, however, your cat may get the notion that the bathtub is a better place for his bodily functions than

FEEDING KITTENS

HOUSEHOLD KITTENS ON LAZY SUSAN

MOTHER CAT TRAINING KITTEN

the litter tray. Leaving a couple of inches of cold water in the tub will quickly discourage him of this unwanted habit.

First Meal

Sometime after your new pet is introduced to his home it will be time to feed him. Select a flat dish or saucer to place the food upon. Some of the deep, rounded bowls sold in stores as cat-feeding dishes are more suited for dogs than cats. Dogs will push their nose into a dish to get every last morsel of food; cats will frequently walk away hungry rather than submit themselves to this boorish act. Any of the ordinary staple foods listed elsewhere in this book will suit your new kitten or cat. A few teaspoons may be enough for young kittens, while a full grown cat may require two ounces or more.

Try to put the dish in the place where you will normally want to feed him, so that he can become acclimated to this every day spot. (This may not be possible if you are confining the cat to the living room and want to eventually feed him in the kitchen.) Don't pester your cat while he is eating. Many cats do not like humans standing around while they are going through such a vital ritual. He will resent it and resent you. Don't force the cat to eat more than he wants, either. His has been an exciting day, and a heavy meal may be too much for him to digest.

Your Cat's Bed

Cats will sleep almost anywhere that is appealing to them. It may be on the sofa, in a corner of the room on the wall-to-wall carpeting, under a chair or even in your own bed. If you are not particularly thrilled over the latter possibility, it is wise to be firm from the beginning. Make it clear he is not to curl up on your bedspread by removing him whenever you see him there.

It is a good idea to arrange a bed for your cat out of a cardboard carton with an old blanket or piece of cloth covering the bottom. The carton should have high sides and if part of the top is left closed, this will be particularly attractive to the cat, who enjoys a dark, warm, secretive lair.

Scratching Posts

Scratching posts, or exercise posts as some cat-fanciers prefer to call them, are a very necessary item. Having one will save a lot of wear and tear of your furniture. They are not so necessary for young kittens as they are for adult cats, but after a kitten has reached four or five months he will want to stretch and exercise and will pick on your dining room table if no exercise post for the purpose is made available.

Many commercial exercise posts are too flimsy or made of the wrong material to be of much satisfaction

HOUSEHOLD PET KITTENS

HOUSEHOLD PET KITTENS

to a healthy cat. Surprisingly, wood, either plane-surfaced or in bark form, is not the ideal material for an exercise post. Probably the best substance is cork, which enables the cat to dig its paws deep inside and to chew off chunks.

The exercise post should be securely attached to the floor or wall. It is a frustrating experience for a cat to stretch onto a flimsy post that topples to the ground under an excess of pressure. This is guaranteed to drive your cat back to the dining room table.

A cat will use his exercise post about four times a day, on the average. Some cats stand firmly on the floor and scratch furiously, while others seem to enjoy stretching and digging their claws into the post. Still others may climb the post as they would a tree. They are all natural showoffs, however, and much prefer some human company watching them while they exercise.

Toys

Once the personality of your pet is understood, it then logically follows that the expensive, often elaborate toys bought by some cat owners for their pets are a waste of money. A cat will be more satisfied with a ball of string, a crumbled piece of cellophane or a small rubber ball.

To the average person it may appear that a kitten is playing as he swats a ball across the room and then pounces on it. But kittens are not really playful, they are merely following the instincts of the hunt. They are dead serious in practicing their feline art of stalking, pouncing and fighting—using the "toy" as an imaginary enemy. Perhaps the most intriguing toy for a cat to play with is the simplest of all—a paper bag. Kittens love to climb into one and rustle around, attacking invisible foes.

HOUSEHOLD PET KITTENS

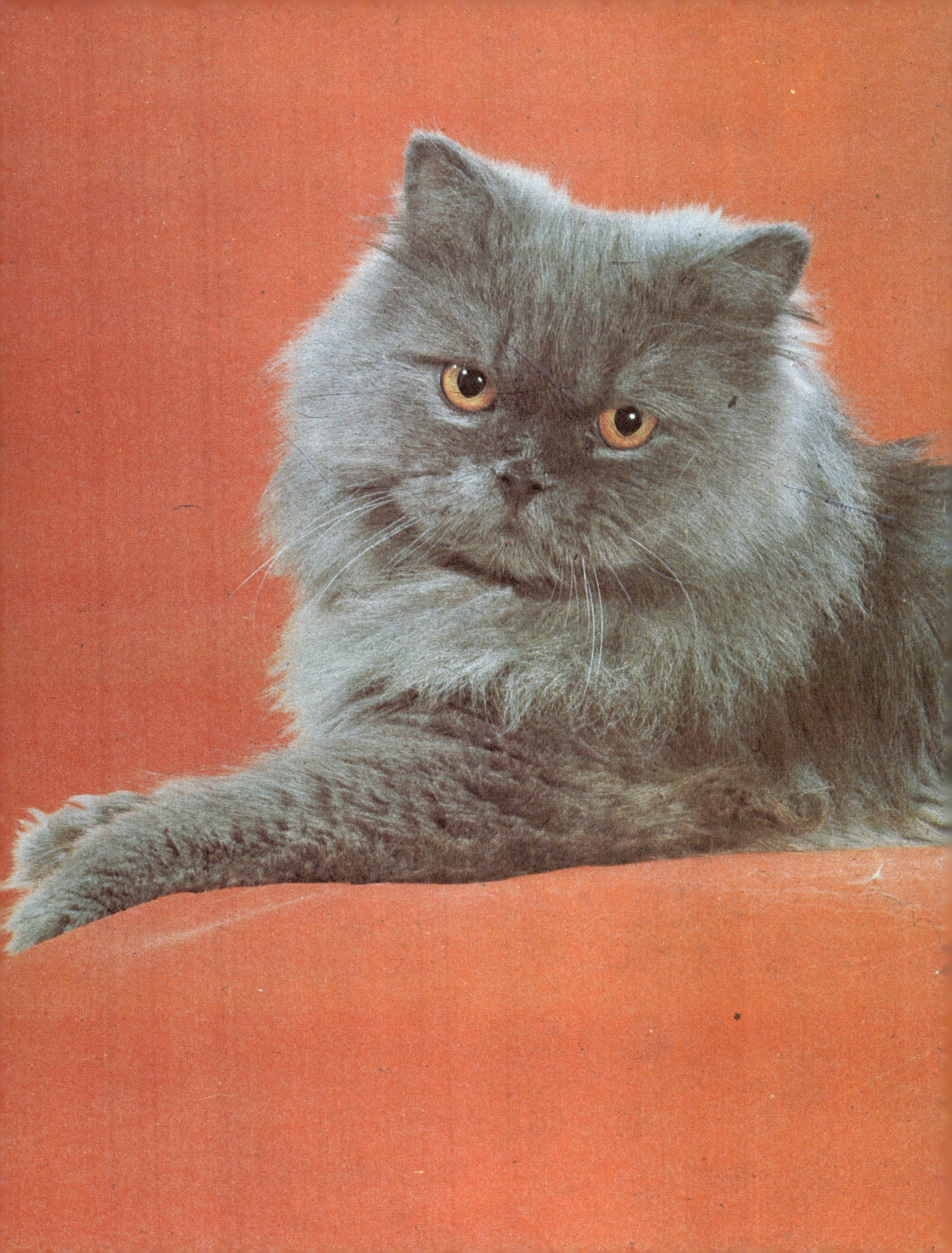

BLUE CREAM PERSIAN

Good Grooming

Cats may not need as much attention as dogs, but nevertheless some care in their upbringing is in order. At the minimum, four duties must be performed periodically:
1. Your cat must be brushed or combed.
2. Your cat's claws must be clipped.
3. Your cat must be bathed.
4. Your cat's ears must be cleaned.

Combing and Brushing

Although cats can frequently be observed licking themselves, this natural cleansing is designed more to eliminate body odors and surface dirt rather than the day-to-day accumulation of dirt that can only be removed by brushing.

Short-haired cats should be brushed every day with a stiff, plastic-bristled brush. Your cat will not enjoy being brushed at first, but if he is started young enough he probably will come to look forward to it in time. You will have to be very firm at first. Place the cat on your lap and grasp him around the back of the neck. Start brushing against the grain of his fur, thus dislodging loose fur. Then brush downward in short strokes, occasionally pulling the loose hair from the brush. Make sure you cover all of your cat's body including the stomach, legs, tail and hindquarters. Make sure you dispose of the loose hair after grooming. If you do not, your cat may eat it and become ill.

In grooming long-haired cats, a special metal comb should be used since a brush doesn't get into the Persian's thick undercoat. If your cat has oily hair, sprinkle a small amount of baby powder through on the coat and rub it in thoroughly.

The entire daily grooming process shouldn't take more than five minutes, and will insure that you have a healthy looking pet with a silkier and smoother coat. It also prevents your cat from swallowing loose balls of hair that may give him stomach trouble.

Claw Clipping

About every 10 days, a cat's claws should be clipped. If this is not done, the pet is liable to rip carpets, furniture covering and your own skin. Also, if his claws grow too long he might be seriously injured when they catch on something as he is running or jumping.

Most cats quickly become accustomed to the clipping ritual. He may not like it at first, but if the procedure is begun early—at about four months, if possible—you should have no problem. Use either nail clippers sold in pet stores or the type found in drug stores and used for human nails. Hold your cat firmly against your body with one arm and the nail clippers in the other hand. With the hand of the arm holding the cat, press one of the front paws between your thumb and index finger. Automatically, the cat's claws will be unsheathed. Making sure you have a firm grip on your cat, begin to clip each claw on the front paws straight across. Clip as close to the upper section,

WRINGING ODD EYE PERSIAN

SOAPING ODD EYE PERSIAN

where the white turns to pink, as you can. Don't fret if you happen to snip too close to the blood vessels within the pink part. You may draw a little blood, but the cat will not be permanently injured in any way. In fact, when blood is drawn from cats for analysis by a veterinarian he takes it from this area.

Clipping your cat's claws can be a harrowing affair, especially if you do not take charge from the beginning. The process does not hurt your cat at all, but he may be scared out of his wits and so a firm but gentle attitude is necessary when he squirms, kicks or howls in protest.

If, however, you do not have the fortitude to perform the claw-clipping ritual yourself, you can always call on the vet. But, as noted, the job should be done about every 10 days, and this periodic trip to the vet's will cost money. Doing it yourself is the logical answer.

BATHING

Unlike dogs, which require baths quite frequently, cats do not. However, they are not capable, as is popularly believed, of thoroughly cleaning themselves with their roughened tongues. Depending on the condition of the cat's home and the outside environment, every tabby should be bathed with soapy water anywhere from six months to 18 months.

Cats don't like water at all, and the mere hint of a bath to come will send your cat scurrying for safety. So you have to be a little secretive about your plans. On the day you plan to give your cat a bath, first clip his claws—this is for your protection. An excited cat, no matter how devoted to his master, is liable to unsheath his claws when being tugged toward the tub. Try to pick a bright sunny day for the chore and select a room or area outdoors where the least damage from excessive splashing will result. Fill a basin, tub or sink four inches full of lukewarm water and pour in a mild soap powder, liquid soap or detergent. Work up a good lather and then go find your pet. Remember, if you have been careful, your cat will have no idea of the ordeal he's about to endure. Bring him into the bathing room and shut the door tight. He is now in your power, but keep a firm hold! As soon as he spots the soapy water he'll know what's happening and all his animal instincts will tell him to flee.

Place your cat squarely in the soapy water. Hold him by the nape of the neck and with the other hand rub the lather well into the fur and skin underneath. Wash all parts of the cat, including the face and tail. If you let go of his neck during this operation, beware: you'll have a room full of flying fur and soap

WASHING AND DRYING

BRUSHING

BLUE CREAM PERSIAN

BLACK HOUSEHOLD PET

suds, for tabby will be fighting all the time to break loose from such "torture."

After your cat has been thoroughly lathered, he is ready to be rinsed. If anything, this is even a more difficult process for both cat and owner. A double sink is a great help, if you have one. Or two tubs. You can wash your cat in one and dip him in the other for rinsing. Despite tabby's movements of protest, make sure you get all the soap out of the fur, particularly around the eyes and ears.

After rinsing, you can dry your cat off with towels if you are able, but he may prefer to shake himself dry. In any case, leave your cat in a warm room until he is dried.

EAR CLEANING

A cat's ears should be checked and cleaned about once a month.

This is not as difficult a task as it might seem to the uninitiated. Use a straight cotton swab with a mild antiseptic, such as hydrogen peroxide. Clean out the visible portion of the ear cavity. Remove all the wax and dirt you can, changing swabs frequently as they become dirty. If this outer part of your cat's ears are heavily encrusted with dirt, chances are that he has ear mites. If you suspect this, take him to the vet's.

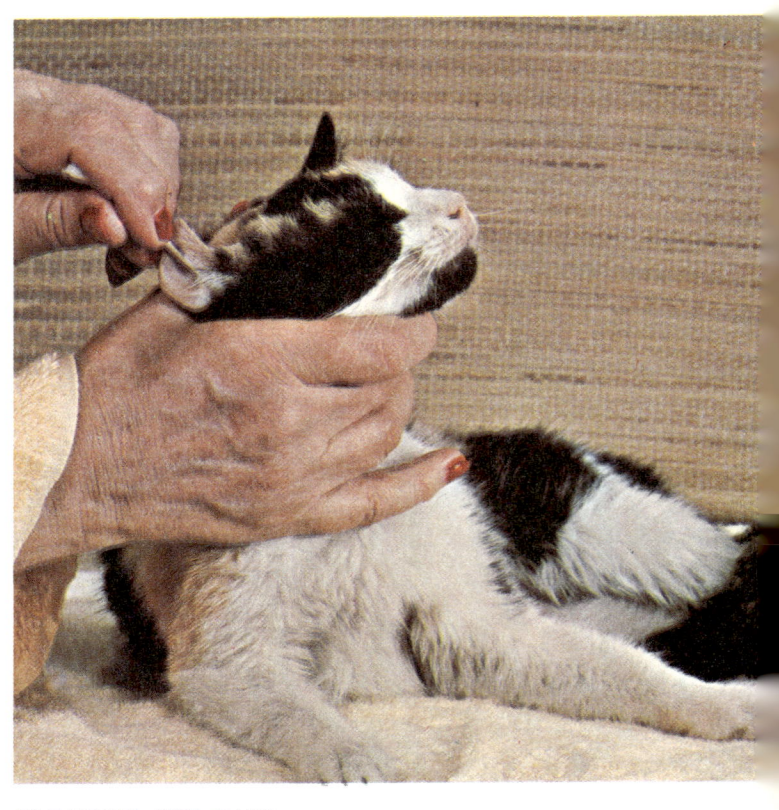

CLEANING THE EARS

After you have cleared away the outer portion, poke the swab into the ear opening as far as you can without applying much pressure. A cat's ear canal is U-shaped, so you cannot damage the ear drum as you can with a human ear. Clean out both ears, of course.

Cleaning the ears is not very difficult if you have the confidence of your cat. But if you cannot control him, it would be best to take him periodically to the vet and allow this professional to perform the task.

OTHER PROBLEMS IN KEEPING
A CAT WELL GROOMED

Generally speaking, cats are quite independent, self-sufficient animals perfectly capable of caring for their own needs. However, they will fall prey to disease, parasites or accident. In many cases, the ability of their owner to help them will determine the success or failure of these outside forces that affect the cat.

For example, your cat might accidentally blunder into wet paint. The cat's natural instinct will be to lick his fur clean, but if there are toxic materials in the paint these may poison your cat. The owner should remove the paint, not with turpentine, but with a vegetable oil that will dissolve the paint. After this has been thoroughly rubbed into the coat, both it and the loosened paint should be washed off with a detergent. If the paint has dried on the coat before it

WHITE PERSIAN

WHITE PERSIAN KITTENS

PERSIAN KITTEN

HOUSEHOLD PETS

HOUSEHOLD PET

BLACK PERSIAN

is discovered, there is nothing to do but clip off as much of the affected hair as possible and wait for it to grow out.

Some cats are plagued with bad breath, but not body odors. If unpleasant smells seem to emanate from the coat, it is probably strong breath odors left over from a time when the cat was licking his fur. A vet should be consulted about bad breath. He can diagnose and treat the cause in most cases. Unhealthy gums, tartar on the teeth, trench mouth, gingivitis, acid stomach—all these can cause bad breath in a cat.

Cats, like dogs, are plagued by fleas. The life cycle of a flea runs from egg to larva to pupa to adult, and this four-stage development makes it very difficult to control the spread of fleas. The female flea lays her eggs on the host, in this case the cat, but instead of staying there the eggs drop off. Many of them land in crevices in the furniture, cracks in the floor, in rug piling and similar places. There, they develop into larvae, feeding on organic debris, and other matter. The larvae are full grown in about two weeks and spin small cocoons in which they are transformed

HOUSEHOLD PET

ABYSSINIAN KITTEN

HOUSEHOLD PETS IN HOBNAIL BOWL

into pupae. In another week or so, the pupae change into adult fleas which go hunting for blood. In many cases, they will seek out any animal—feline, canine or human—to satisfy their thirst.

Many insecticides and flea powders used to rid dogs of fleas are unsafe for cats because these animals constantly are licking their fur and will swallow the poison designated for the fleas. But there are several good flea powders that are safe and effective for cats. When de-fleaing, be sure to spray an insecticide around the floors and furniture to kill off the larvae and pupae as well.

Sometimes cats contract certain skin diseases which can cause humans discomfort if they are spread to them. Fortunately, these diseases are not prevalent among cats but nevertheless they do occur. Among diseases to watch for are ringworm, which is caused by a fungus similar to that which gives us athlete's foot. This is a highly contagious disease. Ear mites, mange, and eczema are other diseases to which cats occasionally fall prey. If you suspect that your cat is suffering from any of these, it is wisest to consult a veterinarian.

FEEDING TIME

Cats are able to take care of themselves, for the most part. They usually see to it that they get the proper exercise and they certainly are among the most hygienic of animals, constantly licking their fur with their rough-surfaced tongue to wash away any foreign

HOUSEHOLD PETS

FEEDING HOUSEHOLD PETS

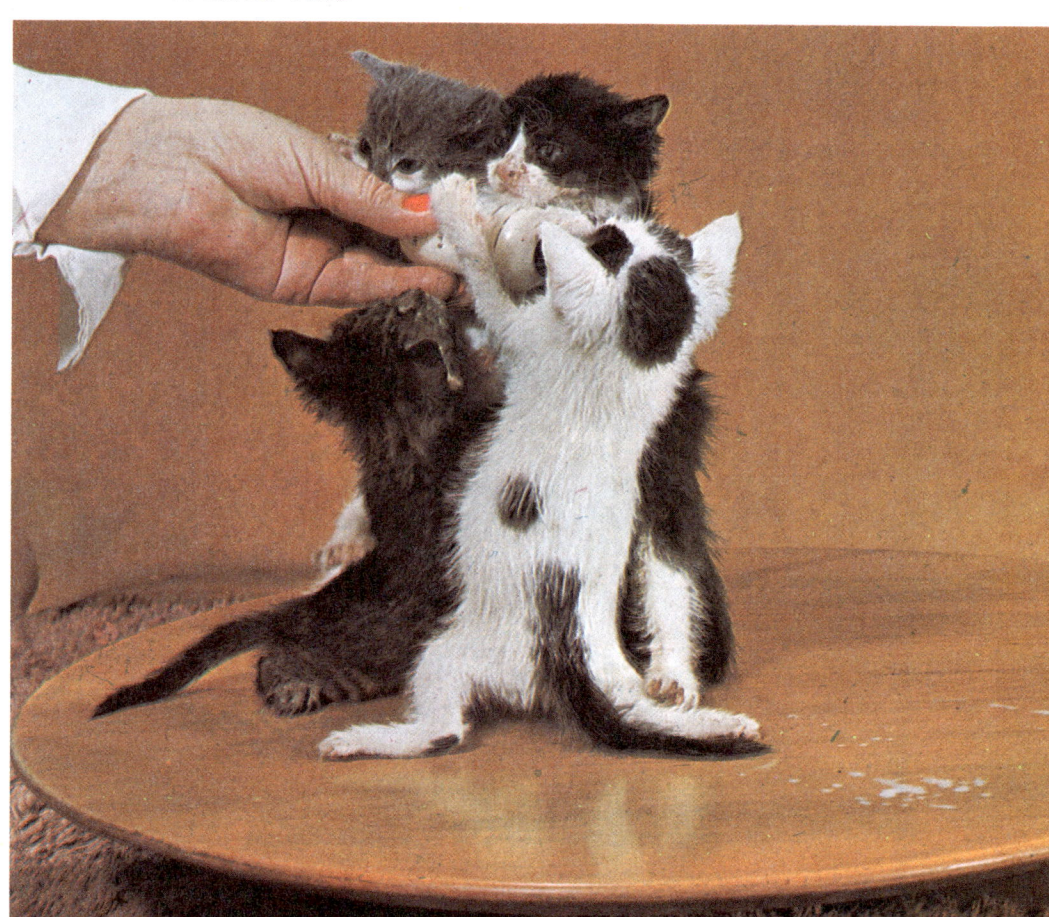

ABYSSINIAN KITTEN

particles. But when it comes to eating habits, the cat needs guidance from his human master if he is to develop into a healthy creature that will enjoy a long, trouble-free existence.

Well nourished cats can live to about 25 years of age. Cats who die after 10 or 12 years often have led a life of poor eating habits. So, a balanced diet and the proper degree of discipline will greatly benefit your cat. The discipline is necessary because cats are such a poor judge of what is good for them. They will eat almost anything, if given the opportunity. They depend largely on their sense of smell and if ant poison is flavored with catnip, they will devour the stuff. Obviously, then, your cat must be protected against his own acute but misleading sense of smell. To him, the leftover roast beef and the string used to tie it smell equally good. The roast beef won't make your cat ill, but swallowing the string surely will.

Many breeders today are feeding their kittens baby food. They find that it contains the vitamins and nourishment cats need to build strong muscle and bones.

Fresh water should be available at all times, as a healthy cat drinks a remarkable amount of water. Milk alone is not sufficient. There are all kinds of vitamins on the market, manufactured with the cat in mind. Supplement your pet's meals with vitamins you find to be palatable to him.

Many companies advertising in cat magazines have free literature available on the feeding of cats. You may also write to cat food companies for suggested diets to best suit your pet's needs.

Protein provides amino acids, "building blocks," required for growth and tissue repair. A kitten's protein requirement is high since this is the period of greatest growth. Milk, meat and cheese are rich in protein.

Kittens normally require a moderate amount of fat for palatability, energy, healthy skin and coat.

Carbohydrates are a source of ready energy. Properly cooked carbohydrates can be digested by a kitten.

Nutrients essential for life and growth—not always provided in sufficient amounts by the kitten's ration—should be supplemented with vitamins. Inadequate intake of these vital substances can cause dull coat, excessive shedding, skin ailments, poor appetite, impaired digestion and elimination, lack of vitality, lowered resistance and other evidence of ill health, as well as subnormal growth and bone development.

Lipotropics—certain vitamins and amino acids are important in the transport of fat in the body. A deficiency of any of these factors may damage the liver, heart and kidneys and reflect in the animal's well-being.

Bioflavonoids promote normal function of the vast network of tiny blood vessels through which the blood carries all the nutrients to the body cells.

Minerals such as calcium and phosphorus are required in proper proportion for building strong teeth and bones; iron, copper and cobalt for blood formation; and other trace elements for nerve, muscle and other body structure.

A kitten's diet consists mainly of milk (canned); slightly boiled ground beef, liver, canned fish (all bones must be crushed); prepared baby cereals; egg yolk; cottage cheese; buttermilk; strained vegetables; and canned cat food of good quality.

Kittens from five to nine weeks old should be fed four times daily. Decrease the amount of feedings to three at age nine weeks to four months. At four months to one year your cat should receive two feedings, and at over one year of age, one or two feedings at regular intervals.

HOUSEHOLD PET

In general your kitten should be fed about one-quarter to one-half ounce of food per pound of body weight per day. This may vary, however, with the amount of exercise and general condition of the individual animal. Don't overfeed your pet and try to space feeding at regular intervals. Your cat should not eat raw pork products, poultry bones, gum, candy, peanuts, popcorn or soft drinks.

Proper diet and eating habits will contribute to the health and well-being of your pet.

HOUSEHOLD PET

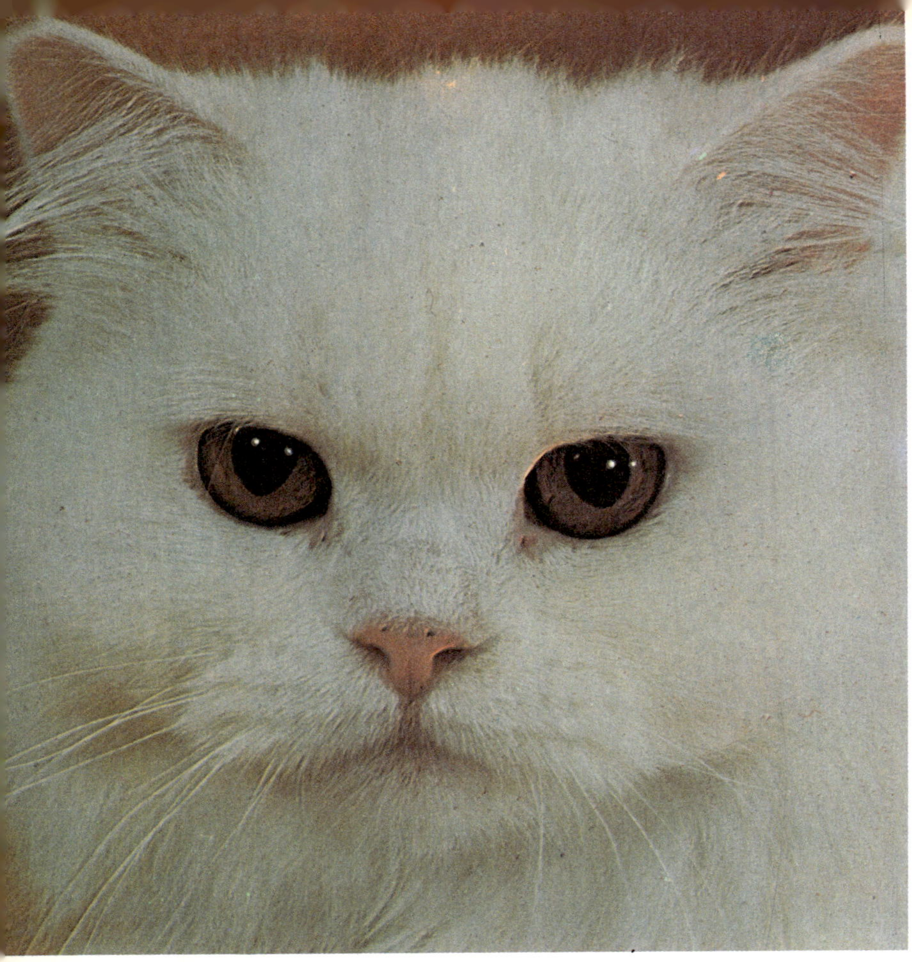
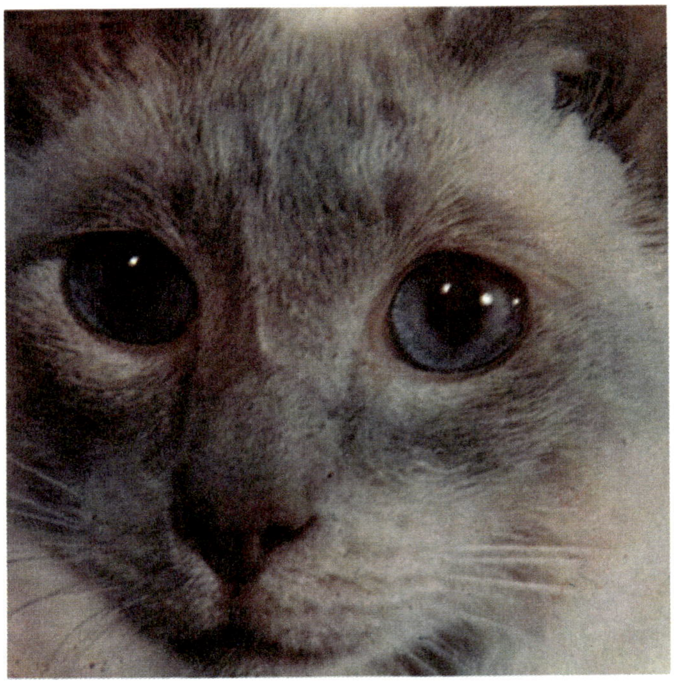
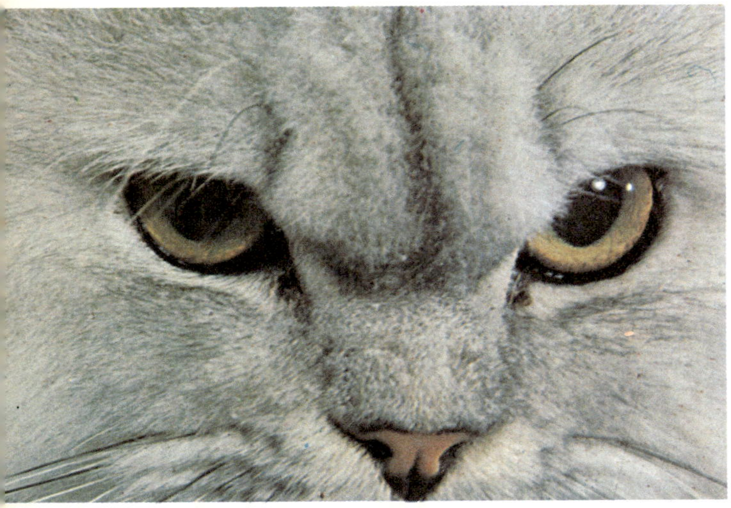
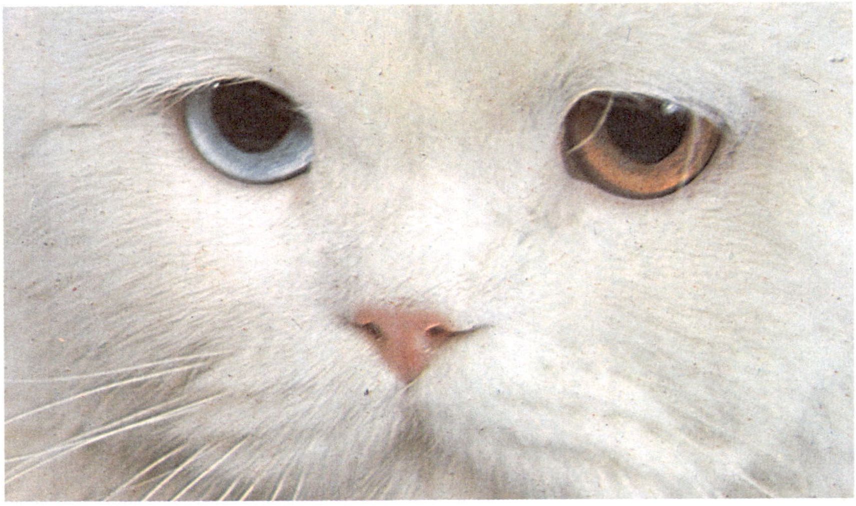
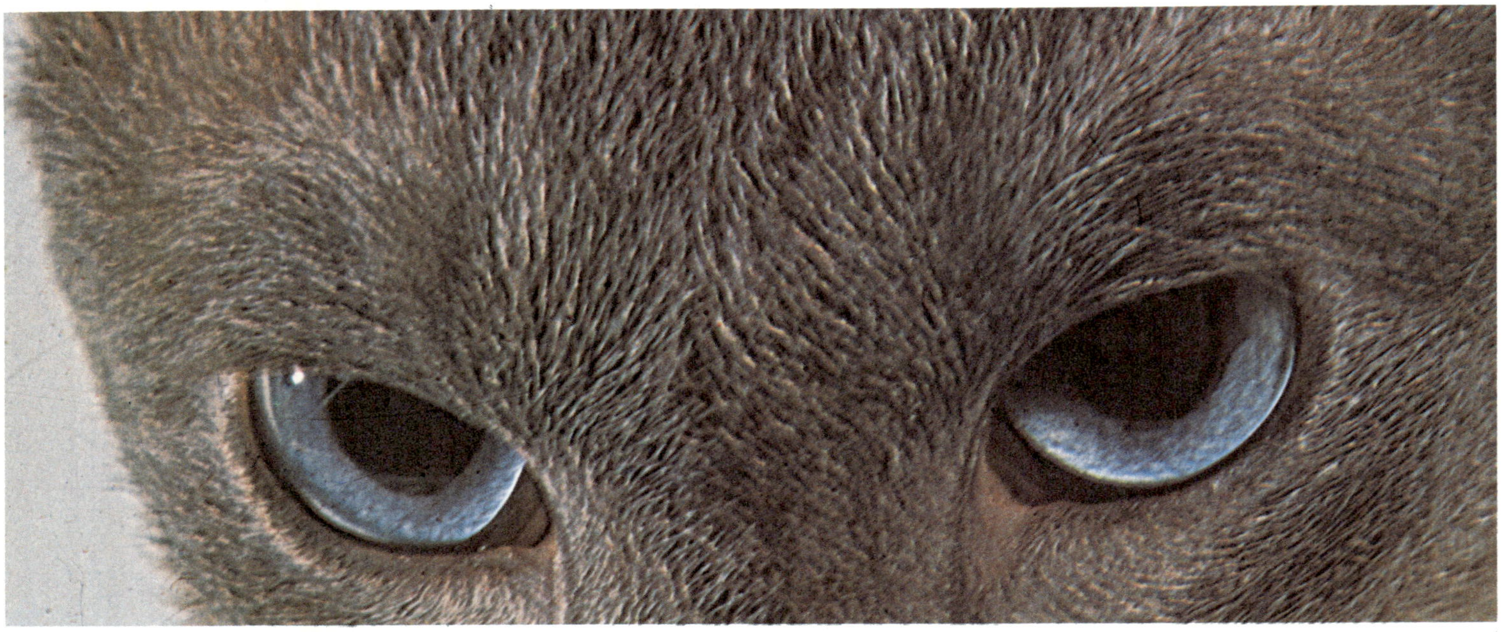

Cats' Eyes

The single most fascinating feature of a cat is its eyes—so spectacular in appearance that they have formed the basis of many superstitions and much folklore regarding felines.

A cat's eyes are quite similar to man's in that they contain an iris, a retina, a pupil and so on. But there are several minor differences. A "third eyelid," called the nictitating membrane, helps protect the eye. This lid, situated in the lower part of the eye, is also an aid to the veterinarian in diagnosing cat ailments since it sometimes will partially cover the iris if the cat has an internal disorder. No one knows just why this occurs, but it does.

Perhaps the most obvious difference between a cat's eyes and those of a human is a special reflecting device that underlies the retina and gives the cat its ability to see well in dim light. This iridescent layer of cells, called the *tapetum lucidum,* reflects light and causes the cat's eyes to shine in the dark.

Contrary to popular belief, however, cats cannot see in total darkness. It is true, though, that the nighttime vision of a cat is much superior to that of man, thanks to the *tapetum lucidum* and an enormous distention of the pupil. The tapetum is a mirror-like surface that reflects light back onto the retina, much as a reflecting highway sign bounces light back when a car's headlights shine upon it. It is believed that this reflecting device in cats enables them to see ultraviolet rays and other light invisible to man.

The eyeshine of cats is not constant, but varies with the individual's eye color, the angle of the light striking it and the exposed surface of the pupil. Depending on the species, a cat's eyes may shine pink, green, blue, golden or red and the color may change when the animal becomes excited.

Cats, then, are able to see far better than man in darkness, and better during the day than many other naturally nocturnal animals such as rats and opossums. But in broad daylight, their eyesight is nowhere near as keen as ours. A cat can see best at dusk, can see well in darkness but can see only poorly in sunshine. A man with normal eyesight can pick out a small object at five times the distance that it becomes visible to a cat.

Cats are also color-blind, or so the majority of scientists believe. Their's is a world made up mainly of gray tones, whatever the time of day. But this color blindness may be fault of the brain, not the eye. It is entirely possible, as some scientists believe, that the cat's eye is able to receive some color stimuli, but the brain simply does not make use of the information it receives.

Veterinary medicine, the science dealing with the prevention and treatment of diseases of domestic animals, is as old as the study of human medicine. The practitioner of this science is called veterinarian, a term that comes to us from the Latin *veterinarius,* which pertains to beasts of burden and draft.

Hippocrates, the father of medicine, considered the pathology of animal diseases as useful information and the histories of ancient Greece and Rome include many references to veterinary medicine. Through the ages, when horses were used extensively in many countries both in peace and war, the farriers, or blacksmiths, often practiced veterinary medicine. In fact, the term farrier was formerly used to mean veterinarian.

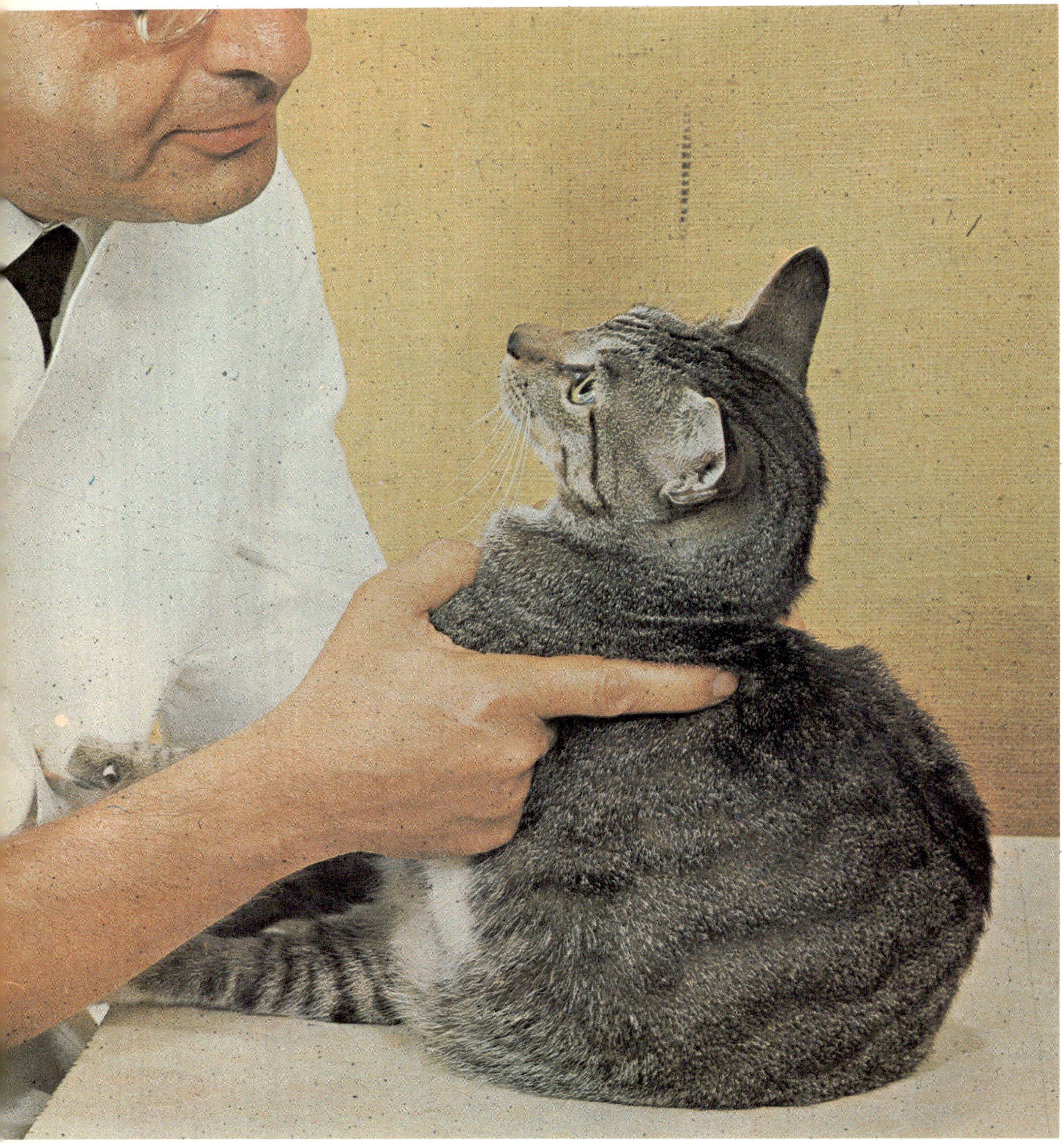

Choosing a Veterinarian

There is much you as a cat owner can do for your pet when it becomes ill, but you will soon find that from time to time you will need expert help. The veterinarian is going to be your best friend in such cases, and you will be wise to choose him carefully.

The time to find a good veterinarian to care for your cat is when you first become an owner. If you have bought your kitten from a breeder or pet store, you should inquire as to a veterinarian. Generally, the breeder's recommendation will be a good one. If you came by your cat through a private party, they, too, may be able to help—but do not put as much faith in their recommendations as you would that of a professional breeder. Should you have become a cat owner by taking in a stray, try calling some breeders or pet shops for advice. A friend who has used a particular vet in the past may also be of help. If no recommendations are available, you will have to pick your vet from the telephone book or some other source.

In any case, you would be wise to (1) interview more than one veterinarian before deciding on your choice and (2) take your cat to more than one veterinarian for an examination. This, of course, involves the expenditure of more money beyond the purchase price of the cat, but will be well worth it in helping you to make up your mind. In visiting each vet and asking him to make a routine examination of your pet you will be able to draw many conclusions based upon the vet's diagnosis and the condition of his place of business.

The first thing to look for when visiting a veterinarian's office is whether care is taken to prevent the spread of disease from one animal to another. The rules that applied to the selection of a pet shop or a breeder also apply to the cleanliness or lack thereof, of the vet's establishment.

The vet's office does not have to be overly fancy or modern, but it must be clean. If sick animals awaiting their turn are permitted to run around the floor of the waiting room, the floor should show evidence that it has been frequently washed. The room itself should be well ventilated. A receptionist, secretary or orderly should be present to make sure that very sick animals are not allowed to run around freely and contaminate other animals. Should an animal perform a bodily function on the floor or furniture, observe closely how speedily the mess is cleaned up.

Once inside the vet's examination room, take note of how carefully the room is kept and what procedures are followed to forestall the spread of diseases. The examination table itself should be scrubbed down with an antiseptic solution each time a new patient is placed upon it, or at least it should be covered with a fresh disposable towel. When examining your cat, the veterinarian should also take care to use sterile instruments and his hands should be scrubbed down before he begins the examination. Beware if your man removes a wooden tongue depressor from his pocket instead of taking a clean one from a package.

Visiting more than one veterinarian will aid you in determining the caliber of man you are going to be

EXAMINING THROAT AND NECK

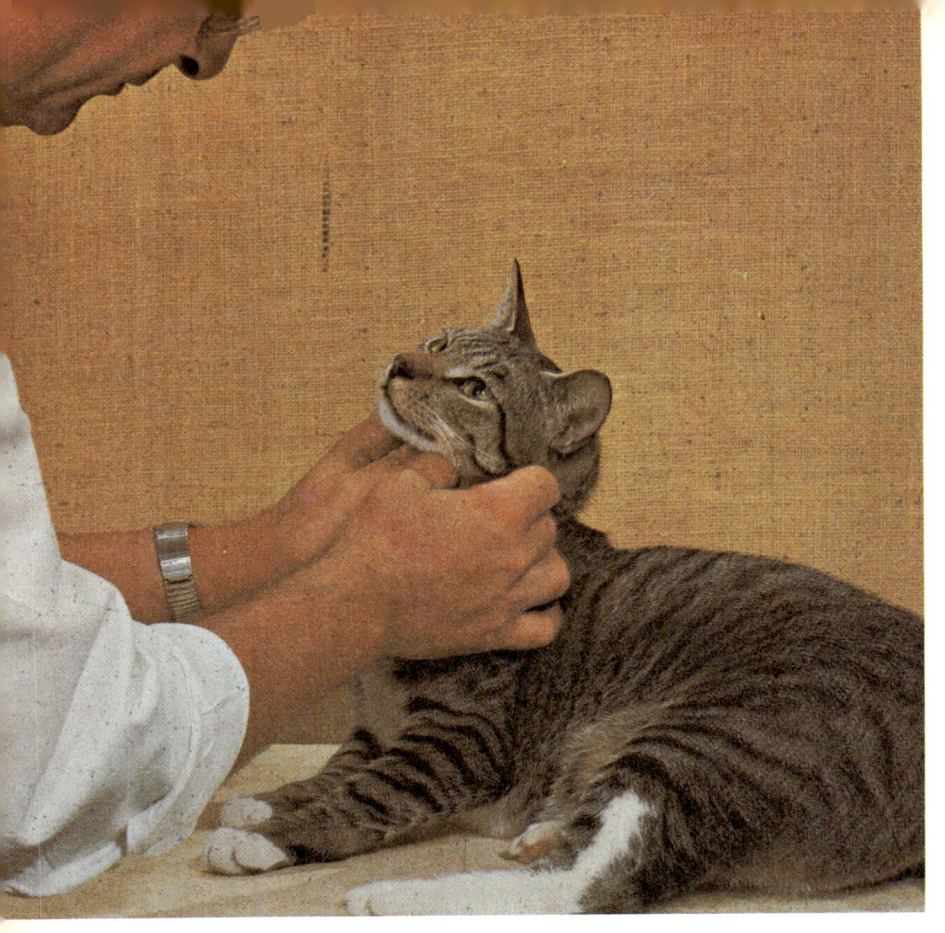

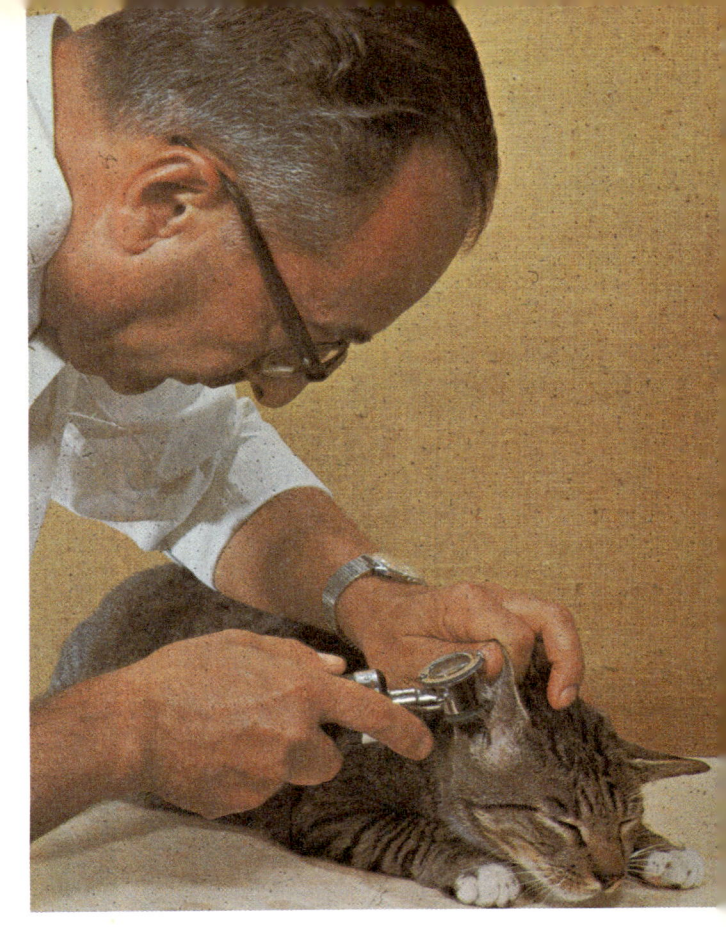

EXAMINING INSIDE EAR

dealing with in years to come. Unlike the conclusions you draw from the man's place of business, which are objective, your impressions of the man himself are quite subjective. This is not to say that he should necessarily possess a good "bedside manner." Sometimes the most friendly, articulate, patronizing professionals are not the best technicians. But in your subjective analysis you should attempt to measure the vet's honesty and integrity. Listen carefully to what he tells you after he has examined your cat and pay particular attention to the manner in which he talks.

If the price of treatment quoted by the vet seems reasonable, you should tell him to go ahead. If, however, the price seems outlandishly high, question the man closely. Ask him what medications he plans to use and what procedures he will follow. If his answers are evasive or vague, you had better leave the premises. Sometimes, close questioning succeeds in bringing the price down.

Prices vary in various parts of the country. In New York, which has one of the highest cost-of-living indexes, here are some typical fees:

1. Routine examination: $10.
2. Neutering a male cat: $35.
3. Altering a female cat: $75–100.
4. Inoculations: $15–20.
5. Enteritis vaccination (two visits): $25–30.

If your cat must be boarded with the veterinarian, the normal charge may be about $5 per day. If medical treatment is needed, the boarding fee is usually doubled. These fees are an approximate average for the New York area and may be more, or less, in other localities.

As noted at the beginning of this section, the veterinarian is going to be your best friend when those occasions arise that you need expert help in the care of your cat. Once you have gotten to know your cat, his quirks and his habits, you will be better able to diagnose whether some unusual symptom indicates a serious illness or just an overnight malady. A slight sniffle, an upset stomach or other minor ailments are usually no reason to rush your cat off to the veterinarian. His condition may be due to any number of factors in his environment such as a change in diet, a dusty floor, an unwanted ride in a car or even the presence of a visitor.

However, if your cat displays some unusual symptom or if an ailment seems to persist more than a day or two, it would be wise to call the vet you have selected and describe the condition to him. He may prescribe some treatment over the phone or request that he see the animal. Whatever the case, listen carefully and follow the advice given you. You have gone to great pains to select the veterinarian you feel is best for your pet—now you must trust him, for he is the professional that knows what he is doing.

If you have chosen well, there should be no problem.

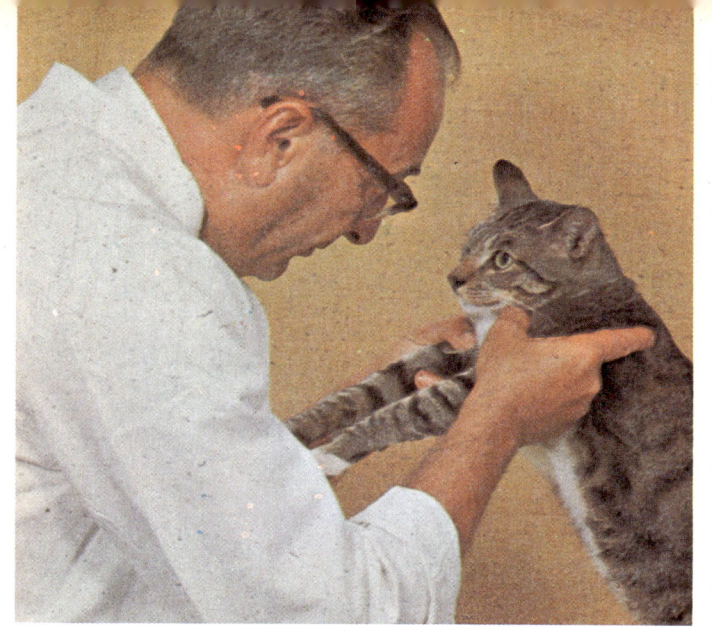

GENERAL EXAMINATION

TAKING TEMPERATURE

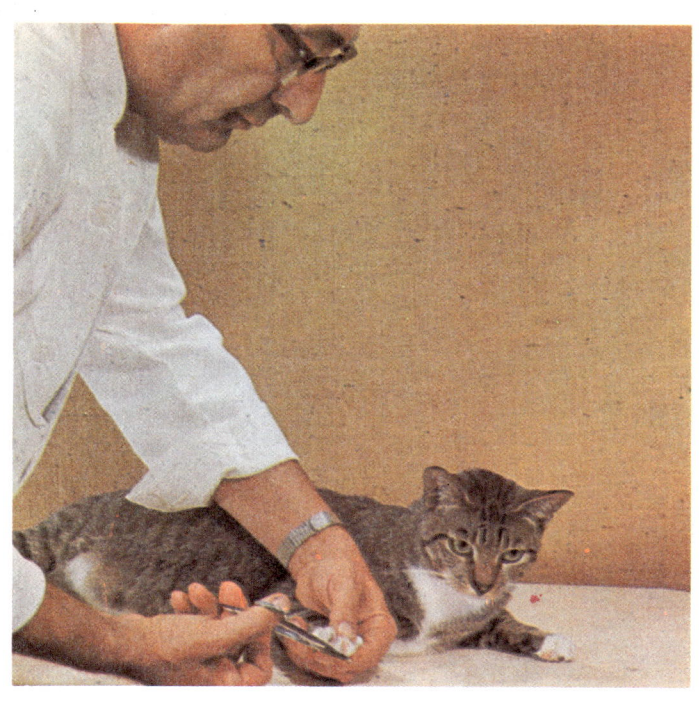

CUTTING NAILS

EXAMINING EYES

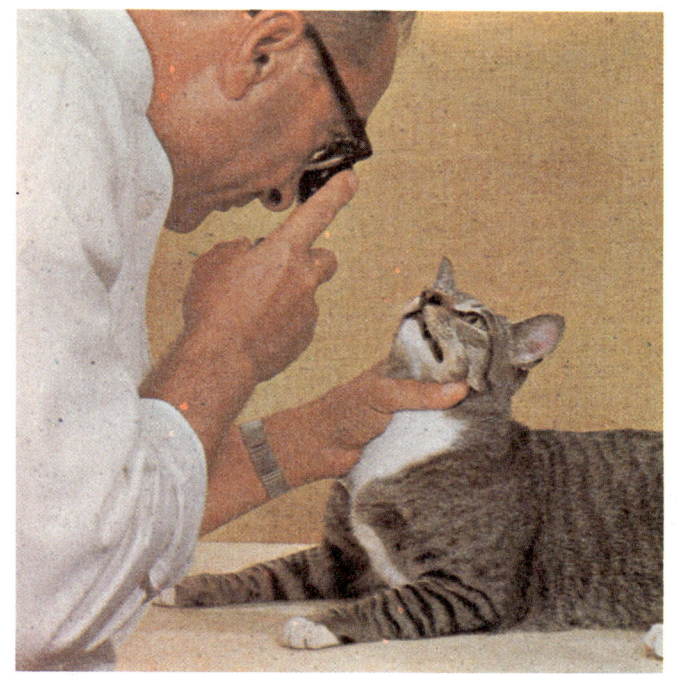

GIVING SHOT

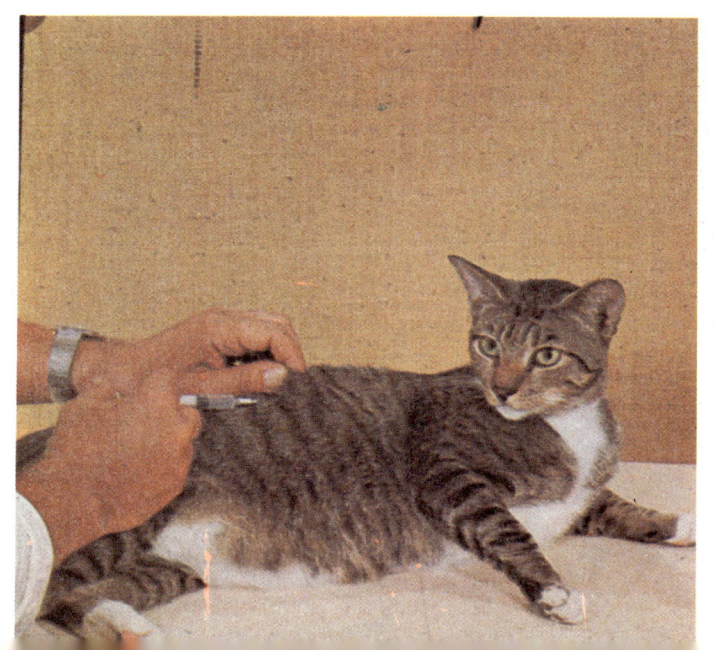

CHECKING HEARTBEAT

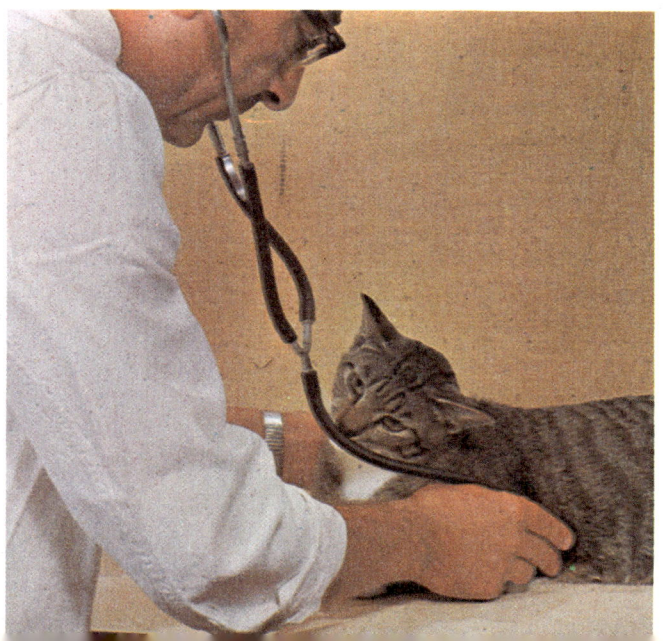

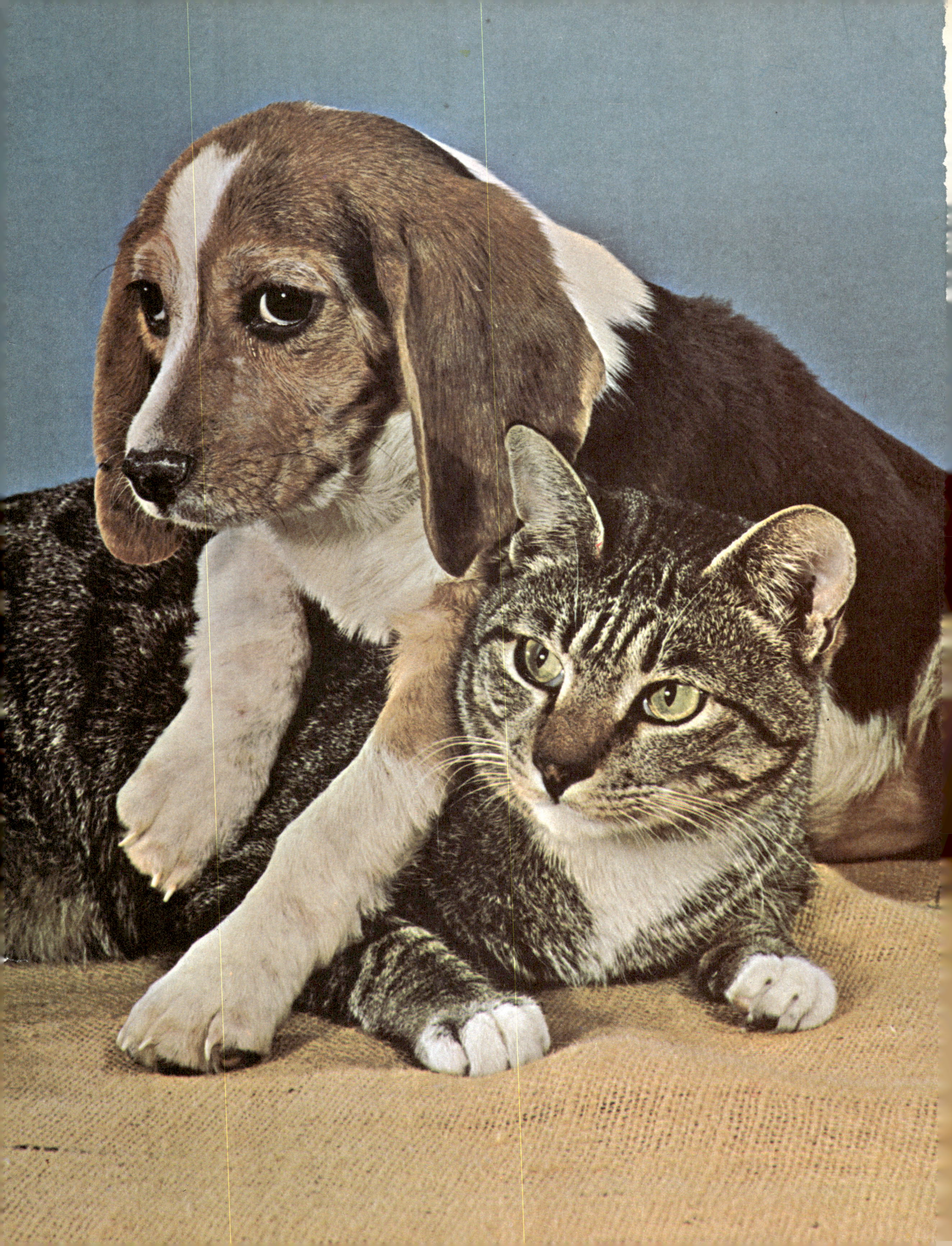

A Cat's Best Friend Is a Dog

Most people think the old saying "they fought like cats and dogs" means that these two animals simply never got along. This is not necessarily the case. Many cats and dogs live together as loyal devoted friends.

In a home where both animals are present from the time they were both very young, the chances of their living together peacefully are quite good. It has been found that they quite normally adjust to each other being around the house.

Keep one important thing in mind, however, during the animals' initial meeting: don't leave them alone until you're certain that the dog is friendly, or at least indifferent toward the cat. You will find that sometimes they merely tolerate each other, and other times you may find them eating out of the same bowl.

Cats, more than dogs, are quite temperamental. If once they are ensconced in a household for a considerable length of time, and another pet is introduced, they may suffer greatly. They can show emotion and have been known to weep. Under such circumstances, many have died of grief.

If, however, an early adjustment to a dog is made, the cat's sense of companionship is strong. Cats have been known to protect unrelated animals and even birds living with them in the same household, yet prey upon the same species elsewhere. They also tend to jealously guard their own mouse holes and home comforts. In time the dogs learns to steer clear of these.

HOUSEHOLD PET

HOUSEHOLD PET

The Outdoor Cat

Your cat may thoroughly enjoy his life of leisure around the house, but even the most docile pet needs to get back to nature once in a while, for it can be great fun stalking squirrels through tall grass, scrambling up trees and pawing at butterflies.

Cats at play, whether indoor or outdoor, are accomplishing a purpose. They are getting needed exercise and at the same time they are sharpening their wits and hunting prowess. They may be domesticated animals, but there is a need to satisfy the primordial instincts. A young kitten is taught by its mother to flex its muscles in preparation for life in the wild. Later, kittens will wrestle, bite, claw and stage make-believe fights with each other for the same purpose—preparation to meet the cruel world. These "games" kittens play constitute attack and defense that might be encountered later on. And the domesticated cat, even more than the domesticated dog, pursues these natural responses.

Many cats that are kept indoors are forced to depend solely on play as the principal form of exercise. When they are kittens, this form of exercise works out well, but the mature cat is liable to avoid such juvenile activity. The tendency then is one of underactivity, which leads inevitably to laziness and obesity.

If you live in the city or in some area where allowing your cat to meander outside by himself is impractical, he will have to be content with periodic strolls on a leash. In mild weather, your cat, if he has been trained properly, may be taken on a short stroll at the end of a leash at any time of the day. Remember, however, it would not be sensible to take tabby for a long walk or engage him in play immediately after he has eaten.

In the winter, if it is not too cold, your cat can also be exercised outdoors. His coat at this time of the year is at its thickest and affords good protection against the elements. This is not to say that he should not be cared for after spending a few hours in the lap of Old Man Winter. Cats sometimes can be so preoccupied in stalking or watching a bird or some other animal, that they may return to the warmth of the house encased in a sheet of ice or snow—and completely unmindful of the fact. They may also be unfamiliar with the treacheries of winter weather and can hurt themselves by slipping off an icy roof or falling from a frozen tree. When your cat comes in from the snow or rain, be sure to dry him off well. Pay special attention to the toe pads because his feet were not made for the type of rough footing he may have encountered.

Summer, too, can be a problem. On the hottest days, you may find that your cat really does not want to spend his time outdoors but would prefer the coolness of the cellar. By all means, if it is practical, let your cat simmer down underground. But don't forget about him and leave him locked downstairs for any length of time. Prolonged exposure to dampness could lead to rheumatism.

Clipping the coat of a cat in summer to relieve him of excessive heat does more harm than good. The coat actually serves as a screen against the sun. Anyway, the undercoat is much thinner in summer than

HOUSEHOLD PETS

in winter—nature's way of cooling off the cat. It would be wise, however, to brush your cat daily to help remove loose underfur. This will help keep your cat even cooler.

In the summer, also, don't incite your cat to play when the sun is high in the sky. Make sure his bed is not in direct sunlight. Most cats will instinctively seek a shady, cool corner to avoid the sun's heat, but occasionally the lure of a favorite chair or outdoor lounge will prove too tempting and the cat will forego the coolness of the shade to sleep, stifling, under the broiling sun.

Should you find it necessary to keep your pet under control, yet not wish to walk him on a leash, the outdoor stake is your best answer. Drive a stake into the ground and slip a stout metal curtain ring over it. This ring should be large enough in circumference to swing easily in either direction. Attach a leash six feet or longer to the ring by means of a swiveled catch. Attach the other end, also provided with a swiveled catch, to your cat's collar.

Now tabby can roam freely within a given radius—play with insects or toys, jump leaves or just nose around in the grass. The reason for the curtain ring is to prevent him from winding himself up on the stake. The swiveled leash catches permit him to turn in any direction without getting tangled. One word of caution, however: do not leave your pet in such a predicament unless you are close by. He would be at a distinct disadvantage should any marauding dogs happen by.

HOUSEHOLD PET

BLACK HOUSEHOLD PET

69

INTERNATIONAL ALL BREED JUDGE RICHARD H. GEBHARDT
HANDLING AND VIEWING A WHITE PERSIAN

Showing Your Cat

Cat shows give serious breeders and owners a chance to exhibit their favorite under the most critical conditions and in competition with other cats of the same breeds. In addition, a Best in Show award is often given to that cat which outshines all others.

For each breed that has been officially recognized by the show's governing council, there is a standard of points adding up to 100. The allocation of these points varies considerably from one breed to another, with the stress given to special features considered to be most important in a given breed. For example, nearly half the points to be gained in the Manx class are derived from (1) a lack of tail, (2) the height of the hindquarters and (3) the shortness of the back. With other breeds, these factors may not be nearly as important as the color of the eyes, the length and texture of the coat or the shape of the eyes.

Probably no two judges will register points in exactly the same manner. Some prefer to note down deviations as they see them while others will take an overall look at the animal and render general opinions. Still others will combine the two methods. Cat-show judges are generally breeders who have exhibited their cats in the past before taking up judging, much like a retired baseball player who becomes an umpire. They are experts in the field and, although they may prefer one breed over another, are usually well versed in all breeds.

Many judges like to view the cats in their pens first, at which time they may make preliminary notes on them. Although this first impression is important, it

WHITE PERSIAN

is impossible to judge any cat without removing it from its pen. This is the point at which the official judging begins. The judge will handle and view the cat from a number of different angles, noting its attributes and faults alike, impartially. If a cat has behaved himself properly during this time, and if he registers well in the judge's mind, he may have scored enough points in his particular class to remain in contention. If, however, the judge has not looked favorably upon the animal, the cat is out of the running. The judging, then, becomes a contest in which the final winner has outlasted all others through several rounds of competition. At most shows, there are two and sometimes three judges who split up the duties into All-Breed and Specialty classifications (long and shorthairs).

When all breeds have been judged there is usually a final grand prize awarded Best in Show or two grand prizes given to Best Longhair and Best Shorthair. Again, this honor is arrived at after an elimination contest involving best male and female kitten and best male and female adult.

PERSIAN

Classification of Cats

No history of the cat would be complete without some mention of the history of cat shows, for which many cat-fanciers spend the bulk of their free time in preparation. The first cat show probably was held in Winchester, England, in 1598, as part of the St. Giles Fair. In the U.S. several informal shows specializing in the Angora were held in Maine in the 1860s.

But the cat show as we know it got its start on July 16, 1871, at London's Crystal Palace. This first major show was inaugurated by Harrison W. Weir. The pace-setting cat show in the U.S. was held at Madison Square Garden in New York City on May 9, 1895. A total of 176 entries were put on exhibit and ribbons, collars, cash and other prizes were awarded. The most valuable cats at the show were two short-haired tabbies, one a male and the other a neuter, each priced at $1,000. Adjudged Best in the Show was a short-haired neuter with seven toes. The Best Long-Haired Cat in the Show were a couple of Angoras, a male and a neuter.

In the beginning, more men than women exhibited cats. But the ladies soon took over and remain the principal exhibiters of cats today. Most cat shows in Europe and in the U.S. are held during the winter because the cats' coats are at their best during this season. At each show veterinarians are on hand to guard against contagious diseases. Generally, a committee is appointed to feed the animals.

The value of cats on exhibit fluctuates with the time and varies from individual to individual. In the U.S., cats have been bought for as little as $1.00 and as much as $2,000.

The Cat Fanciers' Association, Cat Fanciers' Federation and the American Cat Association list more than 130 member clubs dedicated to the breeding and showing of all kinds of cats. The Siamese Cat Society of America, the oldest club dealing with this particular breed, is an independent organization. These organizations issue stud books and registration blanks for the purpose of properly identifying cats and establishing pedigrees. When a cat owner registers the name of a cat, that name cannot be registered by any other owner.

At a cat show, the animals are divided into classes covering kittens, neuters and spays, cats that have not won a blue ribbon and so on. In order of importance, the ribbons awarded are colored blue, red, yellow and green. A Grand Champion and Grand Champion of Opposite Sex are awarded a purple ribbon or rosette. Sometimes a white ribbon is awarded as a special prize. There are separate standards for long-haired cats and shorthairs, covering 100 points.

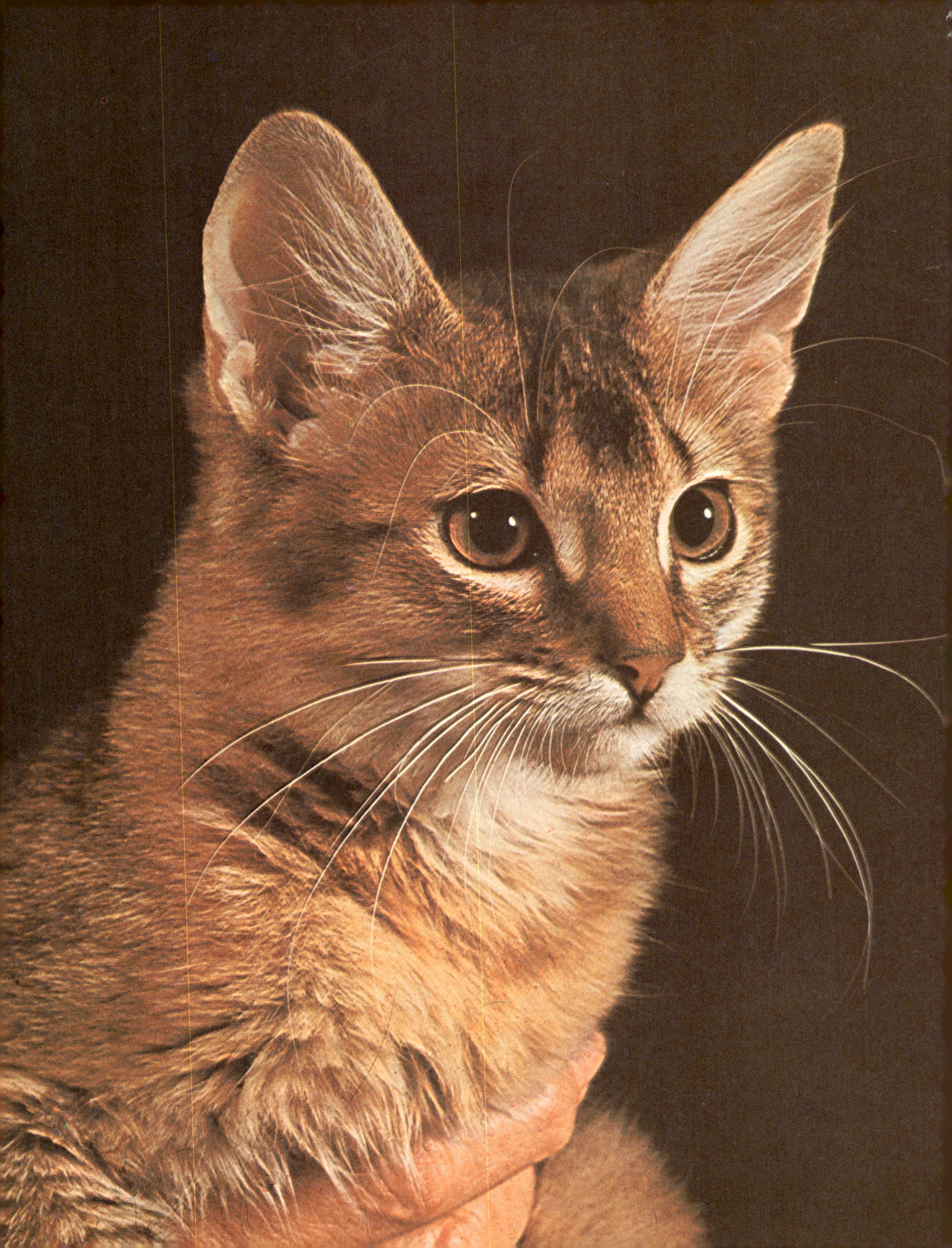

The Abyssinian Cat

SCALE OF POINTS

HEAD	10
EARS	5
EYE SHAPE	5
BODY	15
TAIL	5
LEGS	5
FEET	5
TEXTURE OF COAT	5
BODY COLOR	15
TICKLING	10
RUDDINESS OF BELLY	5
EYE COLOR	5
CONDITION AND BALANCE	10
TOTAL POINTS	100

GENERAL

The Abyssinian cat, or Aby for short, comes closer to the wild cats than any other domestic breed. He is stubborn, primitive, sometimes wild and undisciplined. Abys were called the sacred cats of ancient Egypt. They have soft, thick, luxurious coats, each hair of which is banded with a darker shade of gray against an apricot base. They are more powerfully built than the athletic Burmese and rely heavily on sharp wits and native cunning to make their way in the world. Although shrewd, they are generally less intelligent than the other shorthairs.

HEAD

A modified, slightly rounded wedge without flat planes; the brow, cheek and profile lines all showing a gentle contour. A slight rise from the bridge of the nose to the forehead, which should be of good size with width between the ears and flowing into the arched neck without a break.

MUZZLE

Not sharply pointed. Allowance to be made for jowls in adult males.

EARS

Alert, large, and moderately pointed; broad and cupped at base and set as though listening. Hair on ears very short and close-lying, preferably tipped with black or dark brown.

EYES

Almond-shaped, large, brilliant and expressive. Neither round nor Oriental. Eyes accentuated by dark lidskin.

BODY

Medium long, lithe and graceful, but showing well-developed muscular strength without coarseness. Abyssinian conformation strikes a medium between the extremes of the cobby and the svelte lengthy type.

LEGS

Proportionately slim, fine boned.

PAWS

Small, oval and compact. When standing, giving the impression of being on tip toe. Toes, five in front and four behind.

TAIL

Thick at base, fairly long and tapering.

COAT

Soft, silky, fine in texture, but dense and resilient to the touch with a lustrous sheen. Medium in length but long enough to accommodate two or three bands of ticking.

CONDITION

Lithe, hard and muscular, giving the appearance of activity, sound health and general vigor. Well balanced temperamentally and physically; gentle and amenable to handling.

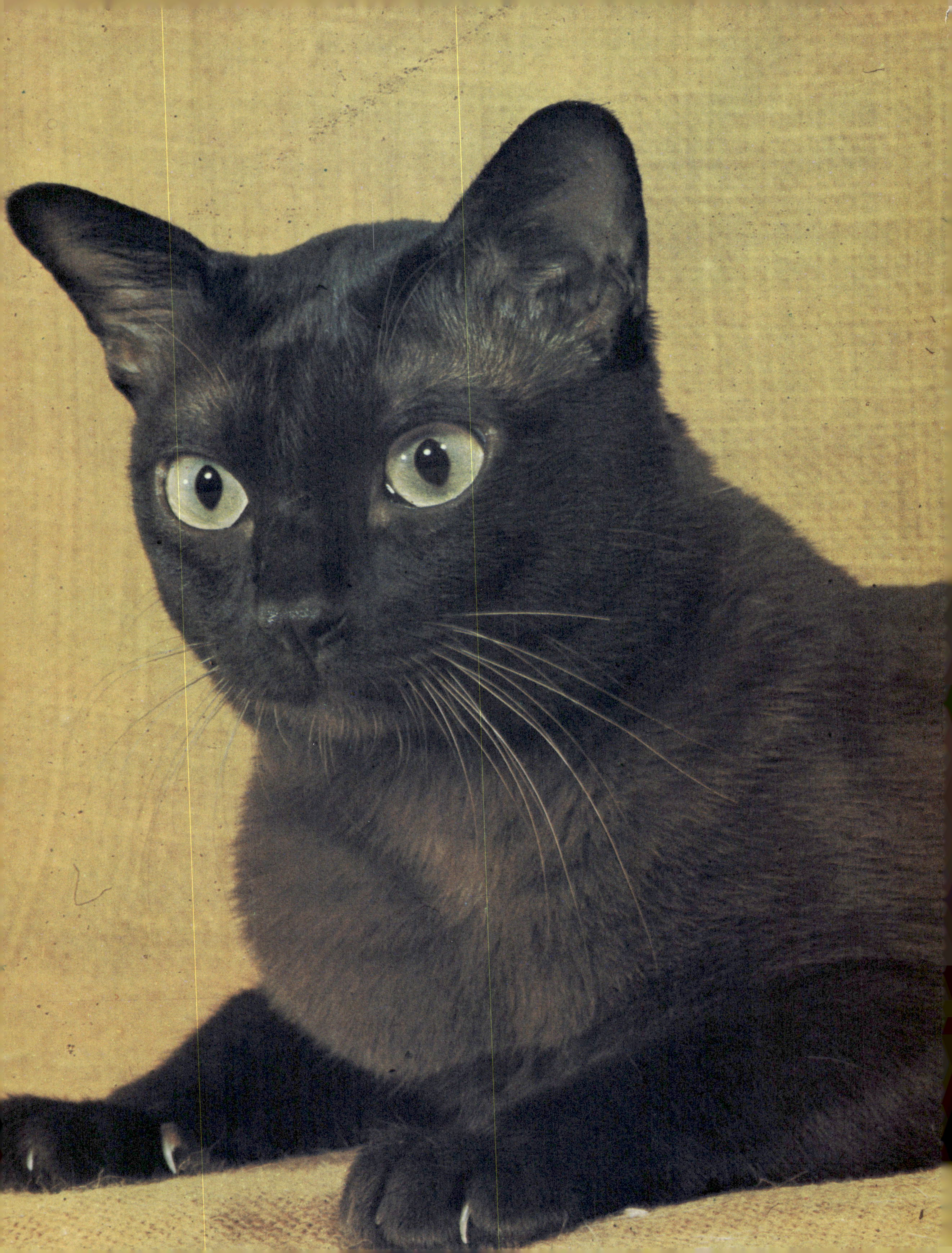

The Burmese Cat

SCALE OF POINTS

COLOR	25
BODY AND TAIL	25
HEAD AND EARS	25
EYES	10
COAT	10
CONDITION	5
TOTAL POINTS	**100**

GENERAL

The overall impression of the ideal Burmese would be a cat of medium size and rich solid color; with substantial bone structure, good muscular development and a surprising weight for its size. This, together with its expressive eyes and sweet face, presents a totally distinctive cat which is comparable to no other breed.

HEAD

Pleasingly rounded without flat planes whether viewed from front or side. Face full, with considerable breadth between the eyes, tapering slightly to a short, well-developed muzzle. In profile there should be a visible nose break.

EARS

Medium in size and set well apart on a rounded skull; alert, tilting slightly forward, broad at base with slightly rounded tips.

EYES

Set far apart and with rounded aperture.

BODY

Medium in size, muscular in development, and presenting a somewhat compact appearance. Allowance to be made for larger size in males. An ample, rounded chest, with back level from shoulder to tail.

LEGS

Well proportioned to body.

PAWS

Round. Toes, five in front and four behind.

TAIL

Straight, medium in length.

COAT

Fine, glossy, satin-like in texture; short and close lying.

CONDITION

Perfect physical condition, with excellent muscle tone. There should be no evidence of obesity, paunchiness, weakness or apathy.

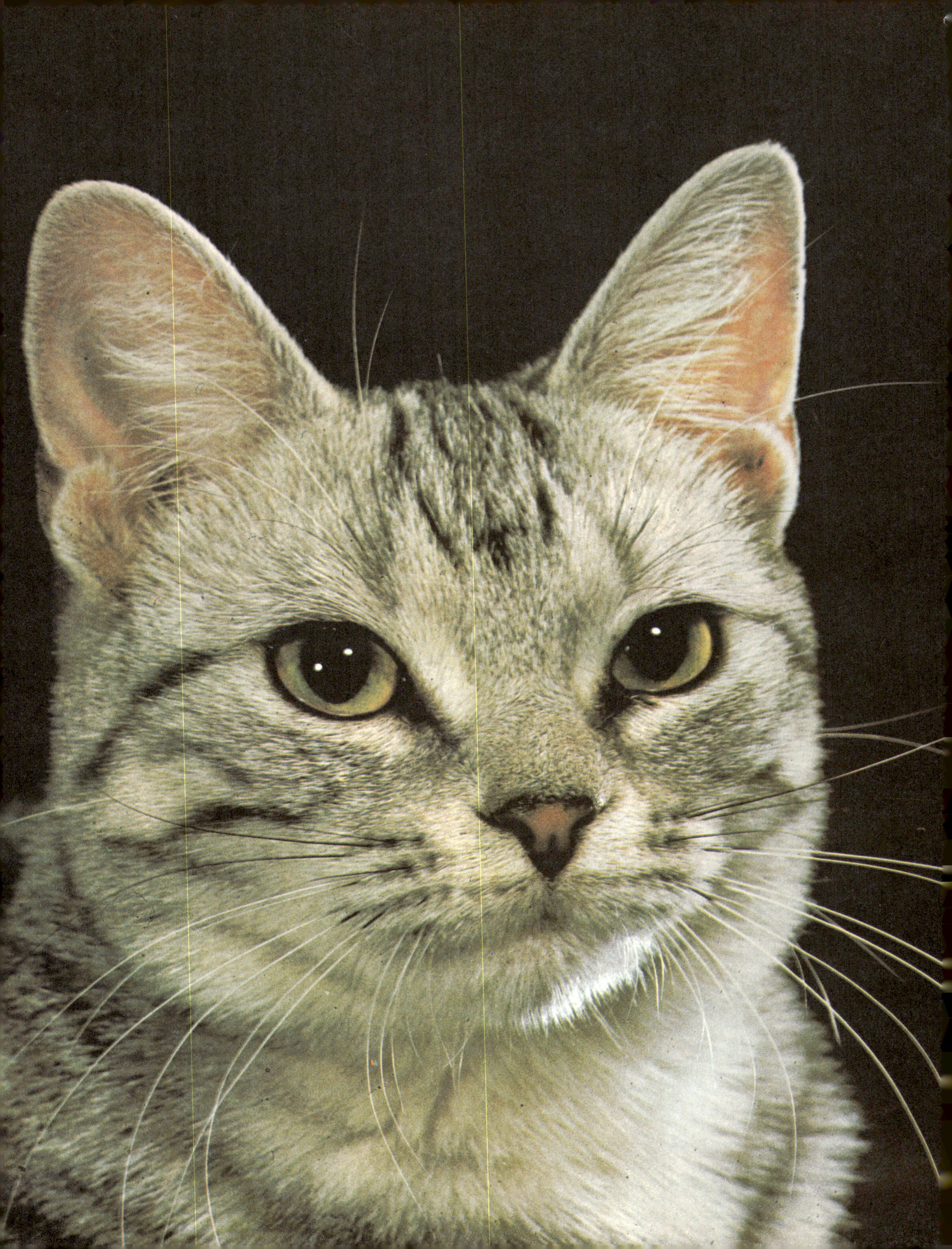

The Domestic Shorthair

SCALE OF POINTS

HEAD	10
EARS	5
EYE OPENING	5
BODY	15
TAIL	5
LEGS AND FEET	10
COAT	15
COLOR	25
EYE COLOR	5
CONDITION	5
TOTAL POINTS	100

GENERAL

The American Shorthair is believed by some naturalists to be the original breed of domestic cat. It has for many, many centuries adapted itself willingly and cheerfully to the needs of man, but without allowing itself to become effete or its natural intelligence to diminish. Its disposition and habits are exemplary as a house pet, a pet and companion for children, but the feral instinct lies not too far beneath the surface and this breed of cat remains capable of self-sufficiency when the need arises. Its hunting instinct is so strong that it exercises the skill even when well-provided with food. This is our only breed of true "working cat." The conformation of the breed is well adapted for this and reflects its refusal to stalk its prey, but powerful enough to make the kill easily. Its reflexes are under perfect control.

HEAD

Large, with full-cheeked face giving the impression of an oblong just slightly longer than wide.

NOSE

Medium in length, same width for entire length, with a gentle curve.

MUZZLE

Squared. Definite jowls in studs.

CHIN

Firm and well-developed, forming perpendicular line with upper lip.

EARS

Medium, slightly rounded at tips, set wide and not unduly open at base.

EYES

Round and wide with slight slant to outer aperture. Set well apart. Bright, clear and alert.

BODY

Medium to large, well-knit, powerful and hard with well-developed chest and heavy shoulders. No sacrifice of quality for the sake of mere size.

LEGS

Medium in length, firm-boned and heavily-muscled, showing capability for easy jumping.

PAWS

Firm, full and rounded, with heavy pads. Toes five in front, four behind.

TAIL

Medium long, heavy at base, tapering to an abrupt blunt end in appearance, but with normal tapering final vertebrae.

COAT

Short, thick, even and hard in texture. Somewhat heavier and thicker during the winter months.

CONDITION

Springy in movement, with muscles lithe and rippling. The framework well padded with hard, lean flesh, giving the general effect of tremendous energy and power held in reserve.

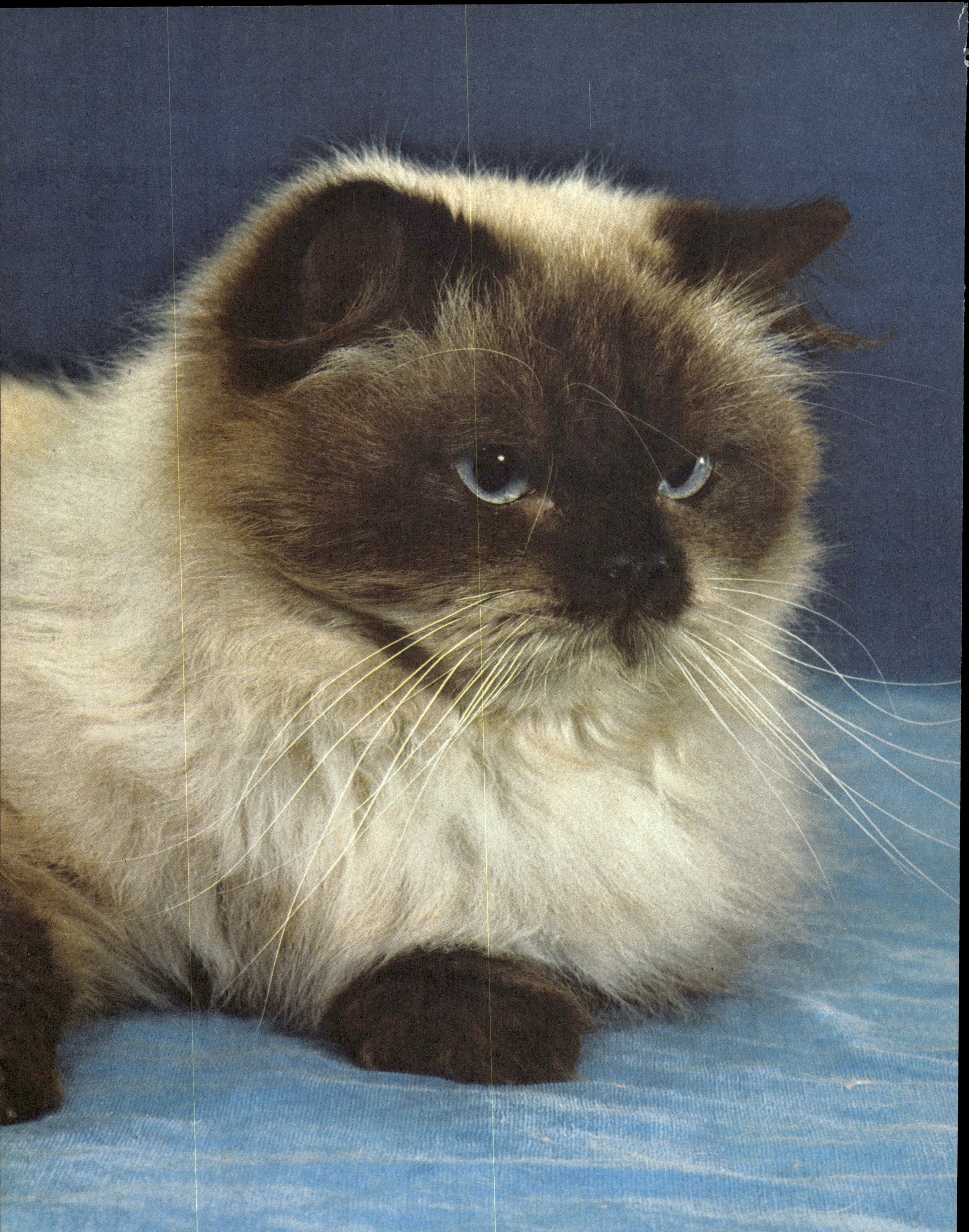

The Himalayan Cat

SCALE OF POINTS

HEAD	10
EARS	5
BODY	15
TAIL	5
LEGS AND FEET	10
EYE OPENING	5
EYE COLOR	5
COAT	15
BODY COLOR	10
POINTS	10
CONDITION	10
TOTAL POINTS	100

GENERAL

Also known as the Colourpoint, the Himalayan is a very popular breed of cat in both the United States and Canada. It has a flowing, creamy coat with various color points. The coat texture is similar to that of the Persian but the color features are more like the Siamese.

Many people mistake it to be a long-haired Siamese, but it is not. Attempts have been made to produce a long-haired Siamese but they have all met with failure. The Himalayan may lose points in a cat show for such imperfection as improper shadings in body color, dark spots, tabby or ticked markings, any eye color except blue, slanted eyes, too long a head, large pointed ears, small feet, kinked tails and crossed eyes.

HEAD

Round and massive, with great breadth of skull. Round face with short underlying bone structure. Well set on a short, thick neck.

NOSE

Short, snub and broad. With "Break."

CHEEKS

Full.

JAWS

Broad and powerful.

CHIN

Full and well developed.

EARS

Small, round tipped, tilted forward, and not unduly open at the base. Set far apart, and low on the head fitting into (without distorting) the rounded contour of the head.

EYES

Large, round and full. Set far apart and brilliant, giving a sweet expression to the face.

BODY

Of cobby type—low on the legs, deep in the chest, equally massive across shoulders and rump, with a short well-rounded middle piece. Large or medium size. Quality the determining consideration rather than size.

BACK

Level.

LEGS

Short, thick and strong. Forelegs straight.

PAWS

Large, round and firm. Toes carried close, five in front and four behind.

TAIL

Short, but in proportion to body length. Carried without a curve and at an angle lower than the back.

COAT

Long and thick, standing off from the body. Of fine texture, glossy and full of life. Long all over the body, including the shoulders. The ruff immense and continuing in a deep frill between the front legs. Ear and toe tufts long. Brush very full.

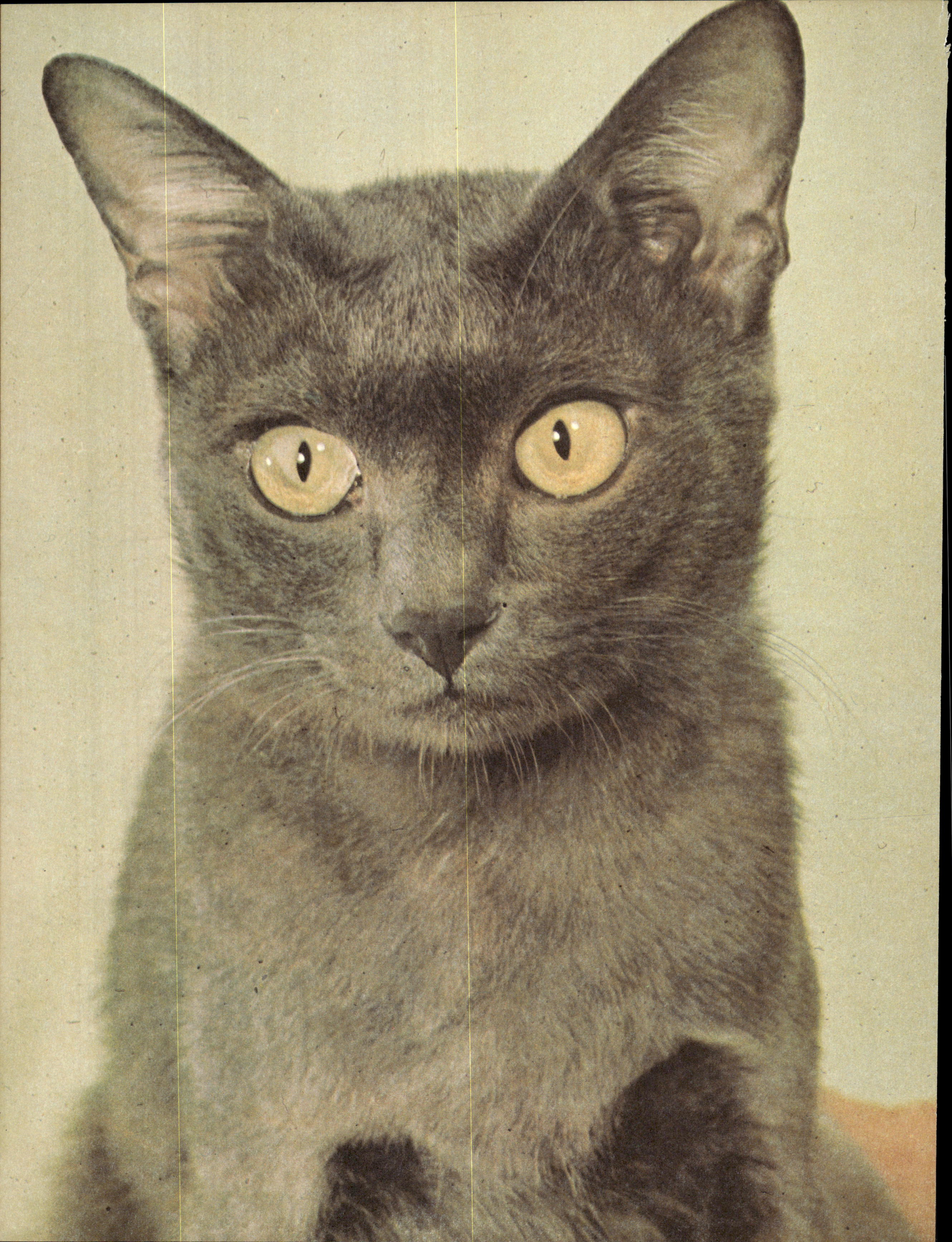

The Korat Cat

SCALE OF POINTS

COLOR	20
HEAD (including ear set and placement)	20
BODY AND TAIL	25
EYES (shape and placement)	15
COLOR	5
COAT	10
CONDITION	5
TOTAL POINTS	**100**

GENERAL

The Korat is a rare cat even in Thailand, its country of origin, and because of its unusually fine disposition, is greatly loved by the Thai people who regard it as a "good luck" cat. Its general appearance is of a solid blue cat with a heavy silver sheen, medium sized, muscular, with smooth curved lines and huge, prominent eyes, alert and expressive.

HEAD

When viewed from the front, head is heart-shaped with breadth between and across the eyes, gently curving to a well developed but not sharply pointed muzzle. Forehead large, flat. In the male there is an indentation in the center of the forehead which accentuates this heart-shaped appearance.

NOSE

Short and with slight downward curve. In profile there is a slight stop between forehead and nose.

CHIN AND JAWS

Strong.

EARS

Large, with a rounded tip and large flare at base, set high on head, giving an alert expression. Inside ears sparsely furnished.

BODY

Medium in size with a strong, muscular, semi-cobby body, medium bone structure. Back carried in a curve.

LEGS

Well proportioned to body.

PAWS

Oval. Toes, five in front and four behind.

TAIL

Medium in length, heavier at the base, tapering to a rounded tip. Non-visible kink permissible.

EYES

Large and luminous. Particularly prominent. Wide open and oversized for the face. Eye aperture, which shows as well rounded when fully open, has an Asian slant when closed or partially closed.

COAT

Single. Hair is short to medium in length, glossy and fine, lying close to the body. The coat over the spine is inclined to break as the cat moves.

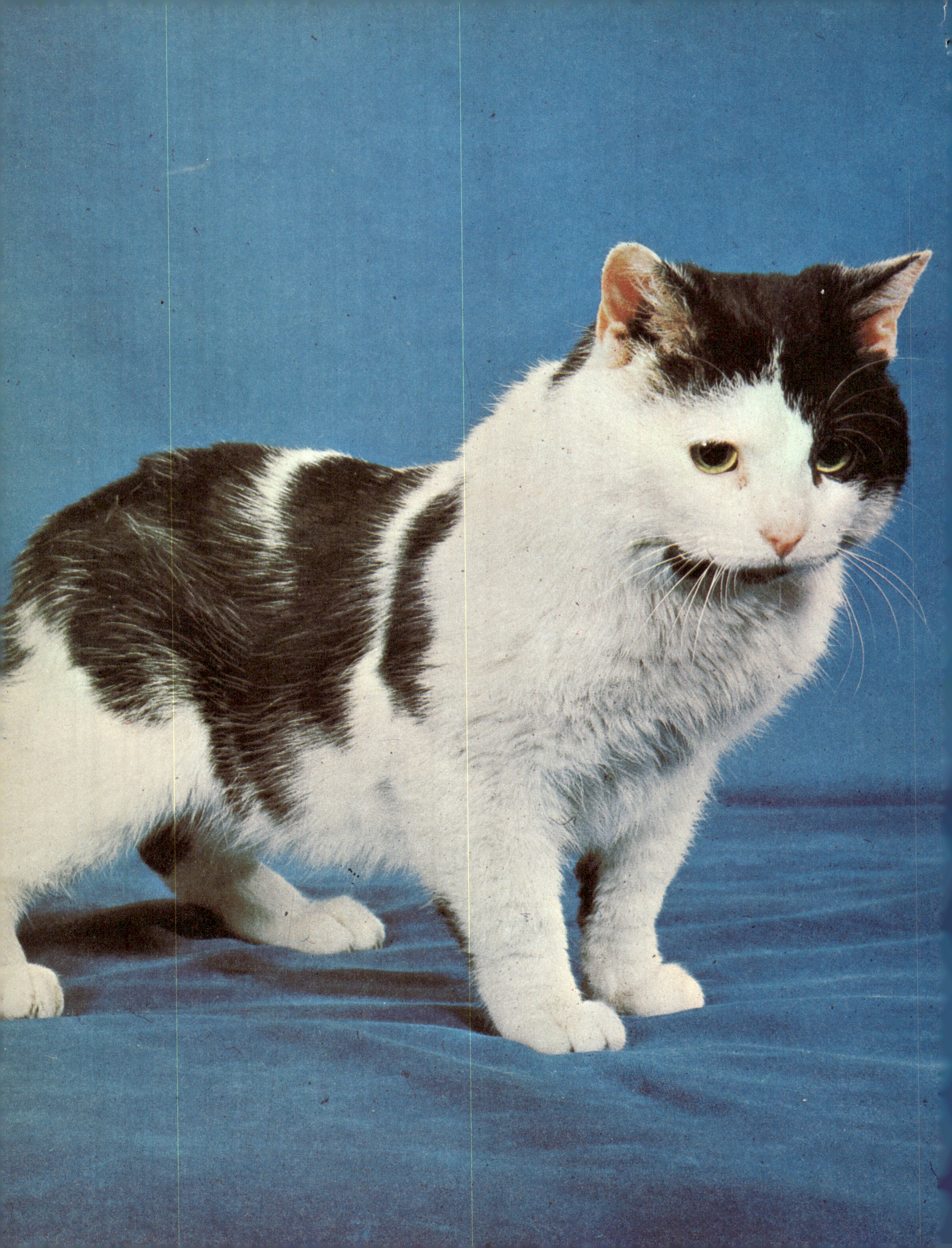

The Manx Cat

SCALE OF POINTS

HEAD AND EARS	10
BODY	10
TAILLESSNESS	15
HEIGHT OF HINDQUARTERS	10
ROUNDNESS OF RUMP	10
DEPTH OF FLANK	10
EYES	5
DOUBLE COAT	10
COLOR AND MARKINGS	10
CONDITION	10
TOTAL POINTS	**100**

GENERAL

A most distinctive cat in appearance, the Manx is born with a complete and total lack of tail. Extremely high hindquarters, combined with short forequarter and the shortness of back in this breed cause an unusual hopping gait. This along with the different head shape and the unusual set to the ears and eyes, give a truly unique "Manx look." Major faults which cost this breed judging points are: short hindlegs and level back; eyes set straight as in longhairs; indication of tail; rangy body.

HEAD

Fairly round with prominent cheeks and jowly appearance. Medium in length without a definite nose break.

MUZZLE

Tapering, but not to a sharp point.

EARS

Rather wide at base, tapering slightly to a point and longer than those of the American Shorthair, but in proportion to the head.

EYES

Large, round, and full. Points to be divided equally between size and color.

BODY

Solid, compact, and well balanced, with the back showing a definite incline from the shoulders to the haunches. Small or medium in size. "Bunnylike" in appearace.

FLANK

Of great length, adding to the cobbiness and balance.

TAILLESSNESS

Absolute in a perfect specimen. A decided hollow at the end of the backbone where, in the ordinary cat, a tail would begin.

BACK

Sturdy and short, to conform with the actual size of the well balanced cat.

LEGS

Of good substance, with front legs short and well set apart to show good depth of chest. Back legs much longer with a heavy, muscular thigh tapering to a substantial lower leg that often has the hair worn off due to the fact that the Manx rests on this part as often as on the paws.

PAWS

Small, neat and well rounded with five toes in front and four toes behind.

COAT

Short, of good texture, with a well padded quality arising from the longer outer coat and the thicker undercoat, known as a "double coat."

CONDITION

Good physical condition. Muscular, good flesh, but not fat.

PENALIZE

A rise of the bone at the end of the spine. A non-visible joint or cartilage.

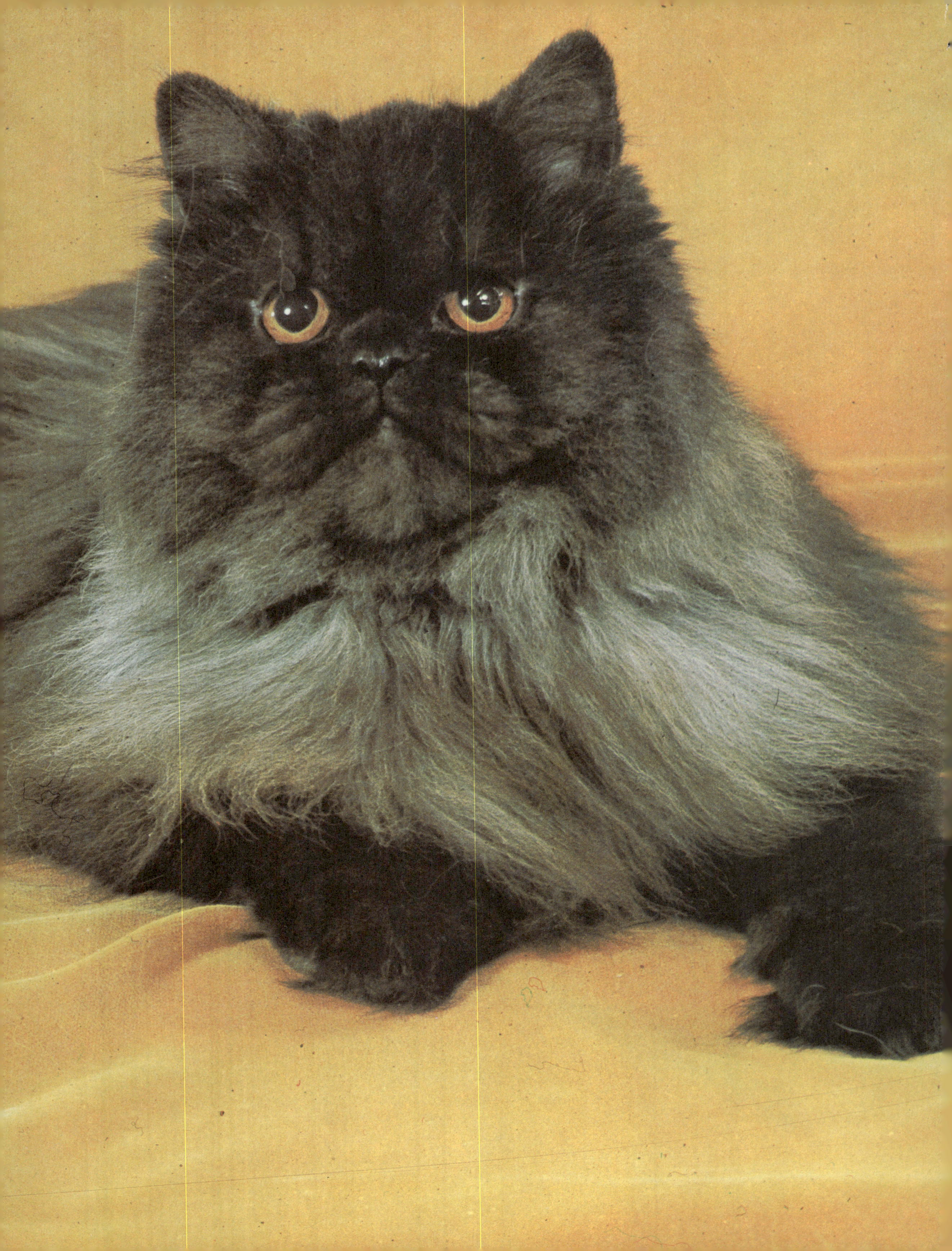

The Persian Cat

SCALE OF POINTS

COLOR	25
COAT	15
CONDITION	10
HEAD (including size and shape of eyes)	20
TYPE (including shape, size, bone & length of tail)	20
COLOR OF EYES	10
TOTAL POINTS	**100**

In all Tabby and Tortie colors the 25 points allowed for color to be divided 15 for markings and 10 for color.

GENERAL

By far the most popular Persian is the blue Persian, thought by many to be the most beautiful of this breed. First imported about 60 years ago, the Persian has replaced the Angora in show standing. Actually, the Angora is no longer shown because of interbreeding with the Persian. The Persian has been imported from Afghanistan for many years, and not from Persia, as many think.

HEAD

Round and massive, with great breadth of skull. Round face with round underlying bone structure. Well set on a short, thick neck.

NOSE

Short, snub and broad. With "Break."

CHEEKS

Full.

JAWS

Broad and powerful.

CHIN

Full and well developed.

EARS

Small, round tipped, tilted forward, and not unduly open at the base. Set far apart, and low on the head, fitting into (without distorting) the rounded contour of the head.

EYES

Large, round and full. Set far apart and brilliant, giving a sweet expression to the face.

BODY

Of cobby type, low on the legs, deep in the chest, equally massive across shoulders and rump, with a short, well-rounded middle piece. Large or medium in size. Quality the determining consideration, rather than size.

BACK

Level.

LEGS

Short, thick and strong. Forelegs straight.

PAWS

Large, round and firm. Toes carried close, five in front and four behind.

TAIL

Short, but in proportion to body length. Carried without a curve and at an angle lower than the back.

COAT

Long and thick, standing off from the body. Of fine texture, glossy and full of life. Long all over the body, including the shoulders. The ruff immense and continuing in a deep frill between the front legs. Ear and toe tufts long. Brush very full.

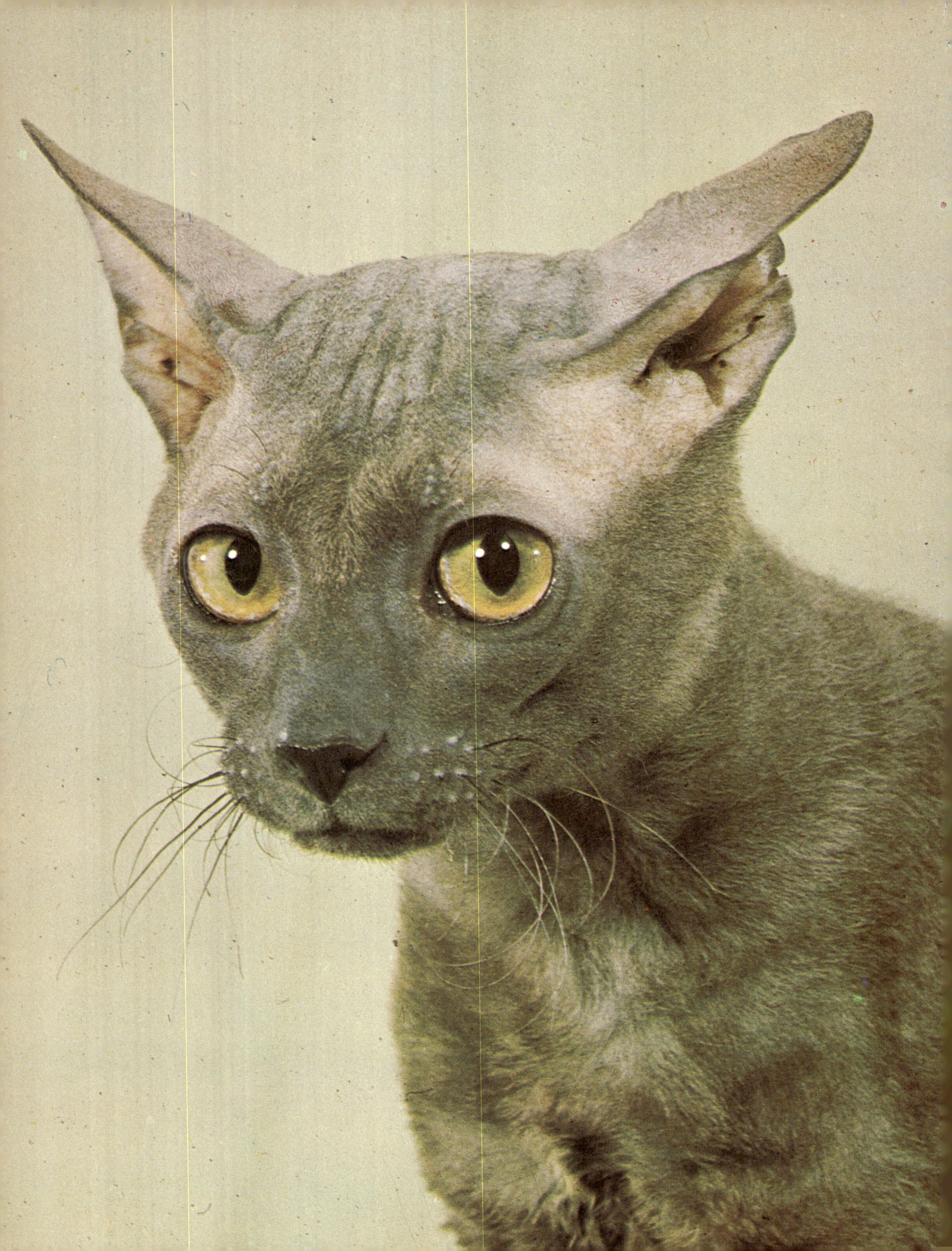

The Rex Cat

SCALE OF POINTS

HEAD:
    Shape, muzzle break   5
    Profile   3
    Chin   2
SUBTOTAL   —   10
NECK   5
EARS   5
EYES   5
TAIL   5
BODY   10
TUCK-UP   5
LEGS   5
COAT:
    Texture   10
    Density   10
    Waviness   10
SUBTOTAL   —   30
COLOR AND MARKINGS   10
CONDITION   5
BALANCE   5

TOTAL POINTS   100

GENERAL

The Rex cat, a spontaneous mutation of the domestic cat, has accentuated the characteristic features of the breed to create a longer, slighter and more agile creature than its ancestors. Its arched back and muscular hind legs develop the flexibility for high jumps, quick starts and amazing speed. At ease its relaxed appearance is contradictory to its capacity for sudden and fast movements. When handled it feels firm and because of its short coat, warm to the touch.

HEAD

Comparatively small and narrow; length about one-third greater than the width. A definite whisker break.

CHIN

Strong, well developed.

CHEEKS

Lean and muscular.

MUZZLE

Narrowing slightly to a rounded end.

NOSE

Roman. Length is one-third length of head. In profile a straight line from end of nose to chin with considerable depth and squarish effect.

EYES

Medium to large in size, oval in shape and slanting upward. A full eye's width apart. Color should be clear, intense and appropriate to coat color.

EARS

Large, wide at base and come to a modified point at the top. Placed high on the head and erect.

BODY

Small to medium, males proportionally larger. Torso long and slender. Back is arched with lower line of the body following the upward curve.

SHOULDERS

Well knit.

RUMP

Rounded, well muscled.

LEGS

Very long and slender. Hips well muscled, somewhat heavy in proportion to the rest of the body. The Rex stands high on its legs.

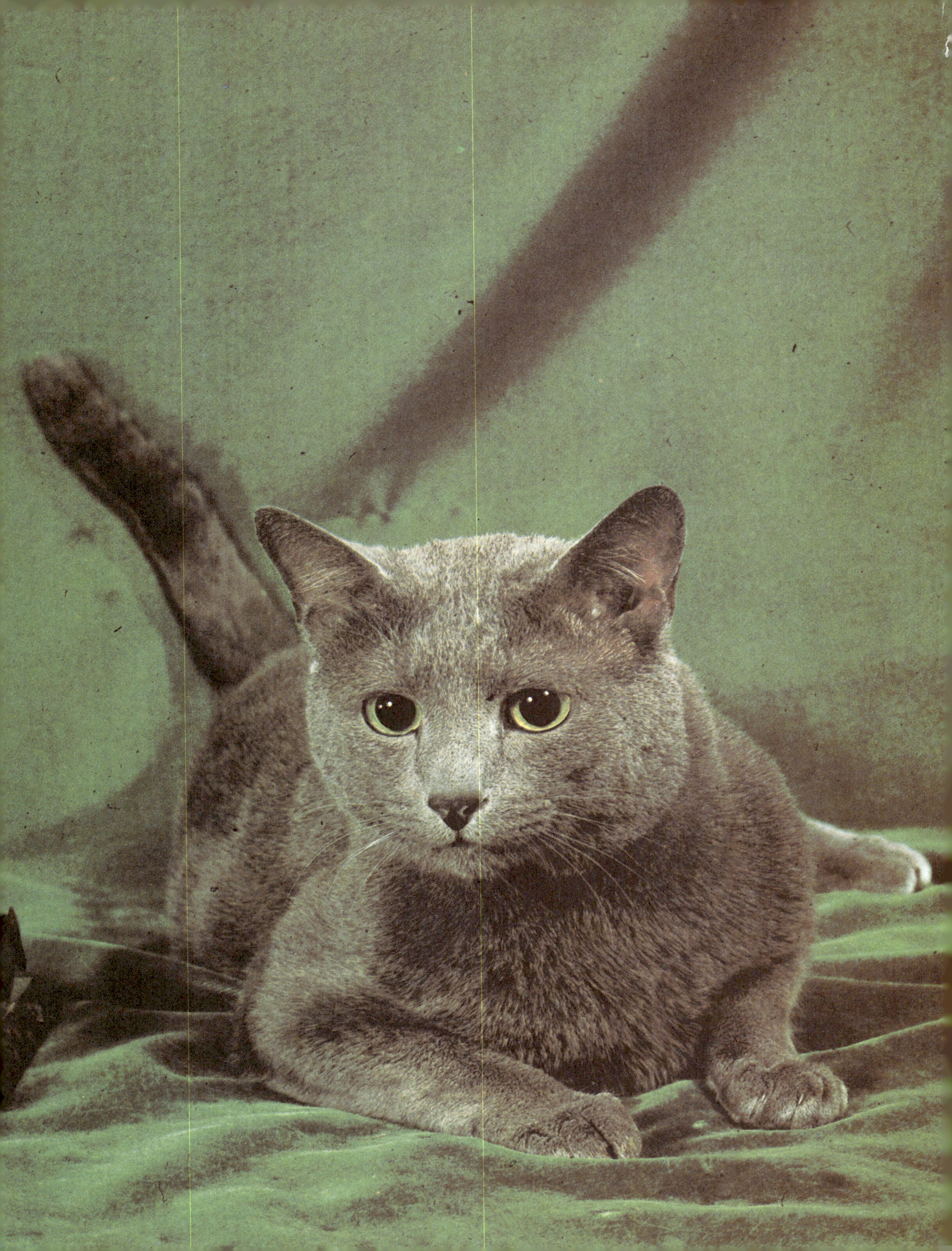

The Russian Blue

SCALE OF POINTS

HEAD	10
EARS	5
EYE SHAPE	5
BODY	15
TAIL	5
LEGS AND FEET	10
COAT	15
EYE COLOR	5
COLOR	20
CONDITION	10
TOTAL POINTS	**100**

GENERAL

A lovely, relatively new breed, once called Archangel Blue or Foreign Blue, with a unique, seal-like double coat—very different from any other cat. The plush coat varies in color from medium to dark blue (considered gray by some). Quiet and royal in nature, this breed differs from the blue Domestic Shorthair by its lithe, long body and soft, silky seal-like coat. Major faults which cost this breed judging points are: tabby markings and shading; white patches; rough coat; thickly-set body; improper eye shape or coloring.

HEAD

Top of skull flat and long. The face is broad across the eyes due to wide eye-set and thick fur.

NECK

Long and slender, but appearing short due to thick fur and high placement of front shoulder blades.

NOSE

Medium in length.

CHIN

Under-chin is level.

EARS

Rather large and wide at the base. Tips more pointed than rounded. The skin of the ears is thin and translucent, with very little inside furnishing. The outside of the ear is scantily covered with short, very fine hair, with leather showing through. Set far apart, as much on sides as on the top of the head.

EYES

Set wide apart. Aperture rounded in shape.

BODY

Fine boned, long, lithe and graceful in outline and carriage.

LEGS

Long and fine-boned.

PAWS

Small, slightly rounded. Toes, five in front and four behind.

TAIL

Long, but in proportion to the body. Tapering from a moderately thick base.

COAT

Short, dense, fine and plush. Double coat stands out from body due to density. It has a distinct soft and silky feel.

CONDITION

The good show specimen has good physical condition, is firm in muscle tone, and alert.

WITHHOLD WINNERS

Kinked or abnormal tail. Locket or button. Incorrect number of toes.

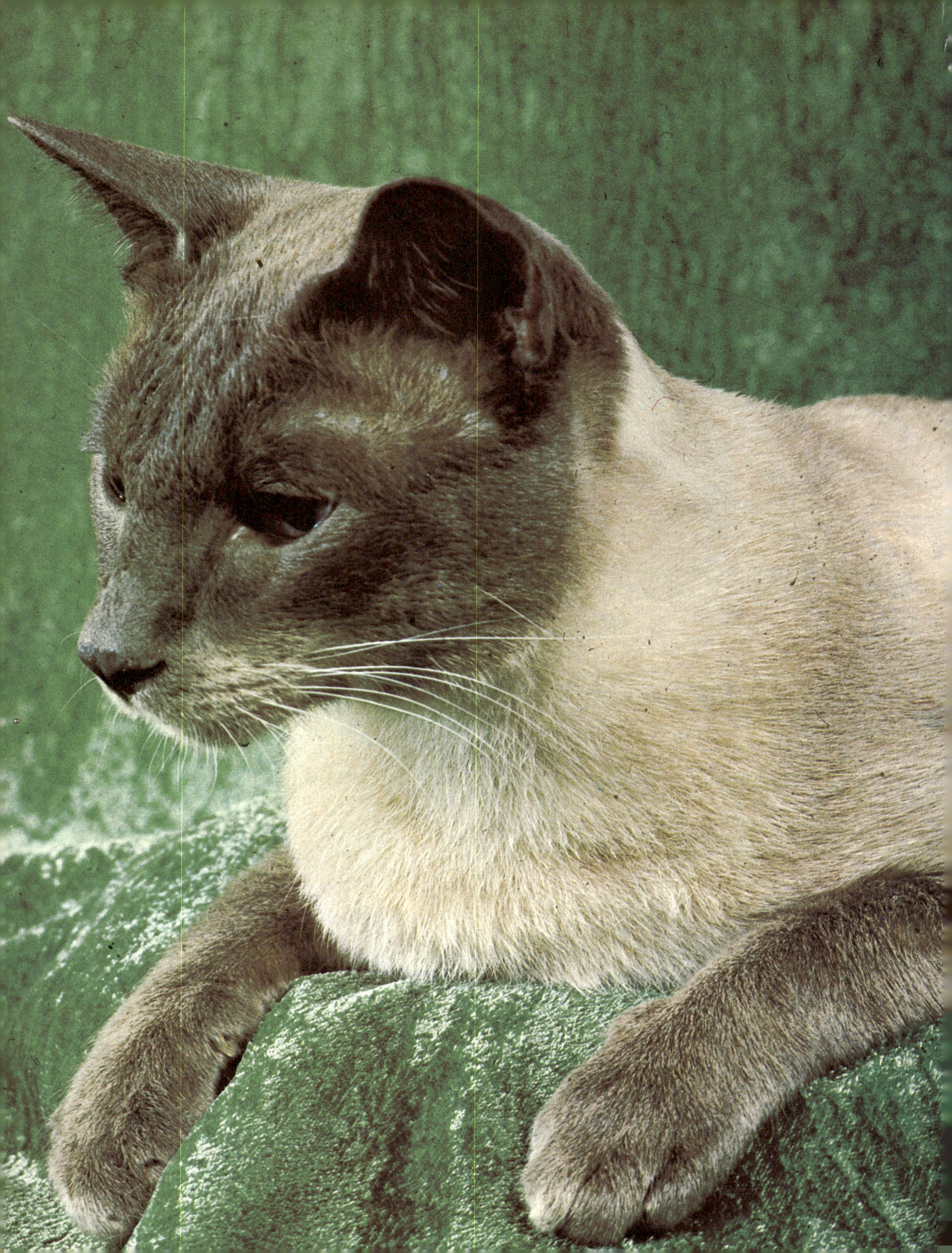

The Siamese Cat

SCALE OF POINTS

HEAD:
   Profile   3
   Wedge   5
   Chin   2
       — 10

EARS   5
EYE SHAPE   10
BODY TYPE   7
TAIL   3
NECK   5
LEGS AND FEET   5

TOTAL POINTS FOR TYPE   45

COAT:
   Closeness of Coat   5
   Shortness of Coat   5
       — 10

EYE COLOR   10

BODY COLOR:
   Tone and depth of color   5
   Shading   5
       — 10

POINTS:
   Depth of Color   5
   Evenness of Color   5
   Conformation to Pattern   5
       — 15

TOTAL POINTS FOR COAT AND COLOR   45
CONDITION   10

TOTAL POINTS   100

GENERAL

The ideal Siamese is a svelte, dainty cat with long, tapering lines, very lithe but muscular. This breed has a distinct personality, like that of a rowdy little boy who gets into everything. Siamese tend to be great talkers.

HEAD

Long tapering wedge. Medium size in good proportion to body. The total wedge starts at the nose and flares out in straight lines to the tips of the ears forming a triangle, with no break at the whiskers. No less than the width of an eye between the eyes. When the whiskers are smoothed back, the underlying bone structure is apparent. Allowance must be made for jowls in the stud cat.

SKULL

Flat. In profile, a long straight line is seen from the top of the head to the tip of the nose. No bulge over eyes. No dip in the nose.

NOSE

Long and straight. A continuation of the forehead with no break.

MUZZLE

Fine, wedge-shaped.

CHIN AND JAW

Medium size. Tip of chin lines up with tip of nose in the same vertical plane. Neither receding nor excessively massive.

EARS

Strikingly large, pointed, wide at base, continuing the lines of the wedge.

EYES

Almond shaped. Medium sized. Neither protruding nor recessed. Slanted towards the nose in harmony with lines of wedge and ears. Placed well within the frontal plane of face. Never at side of head. Uncrossed.

BODY

Medium size. Dainty, long, and svelte. A distinctive combination of fine bones and firm muscles. Shoulders and hips continue same sleek lines of body. Hips never wider than shoulders. No flaring of lower ribs. Abdomen tight.

NECK

Long and slender.

LEGS

Long and slim. Hind legs higher than front.

SHADED SILVER PERSIAN

Glossary

Abyssinian Cat—Purported sacred cats of ancient Egypt. They have soft, thick, luxurious coats, apricot-colored underneath with each individual hair banded with a darker shade of gray, giving an overall ruddy brown appearance. They have triangular faces with glowing orange eyes. They are the most powerfully built of the domestic cats.
Alley Cat—A common shorthair domestic cat that lacks pure breeding.
Altering—Sterilization of a male cat.
Angora—A Persian with unknown breeding background.
Archangel Cat—A wild cat of northern Russia, which gave rise to the Russian Blue.

* * *

Belling—Placing a bell on a cat's collar, to discourage him from stalking birds. However, generally speaking, birds are more than a match for cats in terms of mobility and alertness, and the bell only succeeds in making a nervous wreck of the cat. It is not advised.
Blue-Cream—A parti-colored Persian cat of these hues.
Blue-point—A Siamese cat with points of soft bluish-gray contrasting with a coat of flat white.
Breeders—Persons who breed, or mate, cats.
Breeds, show standards—Cats which exhibit the rigid qualities as devised by the Cat Fanciers' Association and other groups.
Brindling—Stripes on a cat's legs which mar what otherwise might be a perfect coat.
Burmese—A cross between a Siamese and an anonymous ancestor brought to this country in the 1930s from Burma.

* * *

Cat flu—See Enteritis.
Chocolate-point—A Siamese cat with points of chocolate brown contrasting with a pale coat.

Color-point Persian—See Himalayan.
Conjunctivitis—The severe inflammation of the lining of the eyeballs.
Cougar—See Puma.

* * *

Declawing—The removal of the claws, such as in the ocelot.
Delusions, Senile—An effect of old age on cats, in which the cat loses its acute powers of hearing and smelling and "sees" enemies that are not there.
Distemper—See Enteritis.
Dune Cat—A rare, wild cat that dwells in the remote desert areas of the Caspian Sea.

* * *

Enteritis—The most agonizing and deadly of all cat diseases; also called feline distemper and cat flu. A virus infection of the lower intestinal tract, it is 99 per cent fatal in kittens and almost as deadly in adults. Enteritis can kill within hours. Inoculations against the disease are generally successful.
Exercise Post—Also called, inaccurately, scratching post. Any upright post used by cats to exercise their claws and stretch their bodies. The best posts are made of cork.

* * *

Frost-point—An offshoot of the Bluepoint Siamese, in which the mask, ears, feet and tail are of an even paler color.
Fungus Infection—An infection of fungus that affects areas of the cat's body where circulation is poor. Scaly symptoms appear mostly around the ears, face, neck and tail.

* * *

Genet—A whimsical looking cat with large, round eyes, a brownish-yellow coat decorated with red or black splotches and a long, thick tail usually ringed in black. These wild cats have been domesticated successfully, but an offensive odor given off by them ruins their value as a house pet.

WHITE PERSIAN KITTEN

Golden Siamese—A Siamese cat with a rich mahogany-colored body and dark points.

* * *

Hair Balls—The formation of lumps of hair on the coat of a cat. Unless a cat is groomed frequently, he will lick at these hair balls and in the process he may swallow some. This will certainly lead to serious indigestion problems.

Himalayan—A breed produced by crossing a Persian and a Siamese, the result being a long-haired cat with the coloring of a Siamese. In structure and personality it is more linked with the Persian and is generally classified with that breed.

* * *

Lilac-point—A rare and costly Siamese cat, similar to the chocolate-point.

Litter—(1) The offspring produced by a female cat. (2) The material used to absorb the cat's excrement and urine.

Litter Tray—A tray (or box) used by housebroken cats.

Longhair Breed—Persians, etc.

Lynx—A wild cat found in Europe, Tibet and Canada. They have a thick, lush, spotted coat.

* * *

Maltese Cat—A Persian with dubious breeding background.

Manul Cat—A wild cat also called the Pallas cat, native to the steppes of Central Asia. About the size of a domestic cat, it has long, fine gray-brown fur faintly splotched with black. It may be the forebear of the Abyssinian.

Manx—A shorthair domestic cat completely lacking a tail.

Margay—A South American wild cat.

Mist-point—A rare and costly Siamese cat, similar to the chocolate-point.

Mites—Tiny parasites that infest a cat's ears.

Mountain Lion—See Puma.

Mousing—The natural instinct of a cat to catch small rodents. Sometimes the cat may eat the animal; at other times he may be content to tease and play with the captured mouse.

* * *

Ocelot—A most popular wild cat that has never been successfully domesticated. It has yellow fur dotted with leopard markings, a small round face and large, round, yellow, green or brown eyes.

* * *

Pallas Cat—Manul Cat.

Pedigree—A cat whose history can be traced back at least five generations.

Pekingese—An offshoot of the Persian in which the flat face of the breed has been carried to an extreme. The name comes from the Pekingese breed of dog.

Pneumonitis—A severe infection of the upper respiratory system.

Points—Dark areas on the face, feet and tail of a Siamese cat.

Puma—Also called the cougar, or mountain lion. A wild cat found in the Western United States. Pumas have short, sleek fur of a single color, generally reddish, but sometimes gray or brown. Their eyes are a brilliant yellow or green.

* * *

Red-point—A rare and costly Siamese cat, similar to the chocolate-point.

WHITE PERSIAN

Russian Blue—A shorthair cat with a heavy bluish coat. Unlike other shorthairs, the coat of a Russian blue does not lie smoothly against the skin but stands away from the body. Their eyes are usually a vivid green. These cats are among the rarest in the world.

* * *

Scratching Post—See Exercise Post.

Serval Cat—A wild cat of Europe, Asia and Africa. Their fur is yellowish dotted with black and the full tail is ringed with black. They have small round eyes, large ears and long legs.

Shorthair Breeds—Any pedigreed cat other than the longhairs.

Show Standards—Qualities described by the Cat Fanciers Association and other groups.

Shows, Cat—Demonstrations and exhibitions of various breeds of cats.

Siamese—A cat distinguished by his extroverted personality and remarkable coloring, set off by points, or dark areas on their faces.

Spaying—The sterilization of a female cat.

Stud Fees—The fee paid to the owner of a male cat for permitting the animal to mate with a female in an effort to produce desired offspring.

* * *

Tortoiseshells—A parti-colored Persian whose coat is made up of three colors: black, orange and cream. Male tortoiseshells are extremely rare.

* * *

Veterinarian—An expert in the care and treatment of animals.

* * *

Weaning—The process of removing a kitten from its mother's breast and accustoming it to eating and drinking from a dish. Usually a mother's milk supply lasts about seven weeks and the kittens should continue to nurse until that time. Weaning should begin, however, before the mother's milk is exhausted; thus, when the time comes, the kittens will be used to eating and drinking from a dish.

Wild Cat, European—An extremely clever and striking animal found mostly in Central Europe. In size and coloring it looks like a large alley cat.

Worms—Parasites, usually nematodes, that infest the intestinal tract of cats.

SIAMESE SEAL-POINT KITTENS